Ferraris For The Road

By Henry Rasmussen

FERRARIS FOR THE ROAD

Published by Motorbooks International
Publishers and Wholesalers Incorporated,
Osceola, Wisconsin, USA.
Copyright 1980 by Henry Rasmussen.
Library of Congress number 80-83330
ISBN 0-87938-117-5.
Printed in the United States of America.

By 1957 several years had passed since Ferrari had built his last dual-purpose roadster, the famous Barchetta. Richie Ginther, who was racing for California Ferrari dealer John von Neumann, suggested he promote the production of another. The idea was passed on to Modena through the U.S. importer, Luigi Chinetti, and in December of 1957 the first Spyder California was delivered. It was essentially the very successful 2600 mm wheelbase 250 GT berlinetta without a roof. The three-liter V-12 was tuned for 260 hp at 7000 rpm using three large Weber carburetors. It could push the 2,700-pound roadster from 0-60 in only 7.2 seconds. The reliable Ferrari four-speed fully synchronized gearbox carried the torque to a live rear axle with the standard lightweight center section. It was positioned by semi-elliptic leaf springs and tubular torque control arms. As development continued on the racing berlinettas, the refinements found their way into the Californias. No fewer than five different three-liter engines, of the Colombo type, were used between 1959 and 1963. Seven rear-axle ratios offered top speeds from 126 to 167 mph. When the berlinetta had its wheelbase shortened by 200 mm, the California was redesigned for that chassis and began another era of very effective club racing. Both long and short wheelbase versions were used in international endurance racing with success, but Bob Grossman's fifth overall at Le Mans in 1959 must be the high point. Scaglietti built fifty each of the two Farina-designed models and each was available for $12,000.

Ferrari's road cars have epitomized the term Grand Touring since he put roofs on his racing machines, and they had been available for a decade when the 250 GT was introduced. Not since Bugatti, had an individual automobile so captured the imagination of the motor sports world. After three years of dominating the GT category in international racing, a major revision was made. To make the cars lighter and more responsive, 200 mm were removed from the 2600 mm wheelbase, giving rise to the name Short Wheelbase or Berlinetta SWB. If you had 14,000 of the 1960 dollars you could have a virtual duplicate of the championship-winning car. Like it, your car would have Ferrari's robust, forged A-arms and coil springs for front suspension. The simple live rear axle with its leaf springs and torque control arms would carry your choice of axle ratios for dazzling acceleration or incredible top speed. With a 4:1 ratio, 0-60 took 6.5 seconds and allowed a maximum speed of 145 mph. A big, four-speed gearbox filled by powerful, non-silent gears with Porsche-patent synchromesh transmitted the 280 hp at 7000 rpm from the three-liter V-12 ahead of it. Like all road Ferraris, it carried three double-throat Weber carburetors. Disc brakes were now standard, too. The SWB was actually built in two versions, with the body in either aluminum or steel. Scaglietti built two hundred Farina-designed cars, of which seventy-seven 2,380-pound competition examples and seventy-five 2,700-pound road examples are accounted for in 1980.

250 GT California 1957-1963

250 GT SWB 1959-1962

A literal translation of "berlinetta" is "little sedan," but in the contemporary jargon of the Ferrari cult it describes a high performance, two-place coupe. "Lusso" in Italian means "luxury." There you have it. It just might be the loveliest form ever put on a Ferrari chassis. Though designed by Pininfarina, all 350 Lussos were built by Scaglietti. The chassis was very similar to the famous 250 SWB, with the 2400 mm wheelbase, but with concessions for comfortable touring. Touring here must be qualified. One suitcase would fit behind the seats. The trunk could hold a couple of sweaters and the fat 184x15 spare tire, so rather short tours would be in order. But however long the trip, it would be accompanied by the melodies of that marvelous three-liter V-12. It was all there, the three Weber carburetors, the singing, triplex timing chain for the single-overhead-cams, and 250 prancing cavalini at 7500 rpm. The precise four-speed gearbox allowed 0-60 in 8 seconds, a 150-mph top speed, and 14-17 mpg could still be obtained from the 2,995-pound car. The front suspension included a substantial sway bar which allowed relatively soft springing with little body roll in cornering and predictable understeer. The rear suspension remained effectively firm. The semi-elliptic springs and tubular torque control arms had to steady the tail with thirty gallons of 50¢ premium fuel suspended behind the live rear axle. Still one of the most sought-after Ferraris, it originally sold for $13,375. A reliable and economical Ferrari for daily use.

"Click! Key on. Click! Fuel pump—tick—tick—tick—tick—tick—tick—tick. Starter—rowrowrow, WHOOM! The first time you start a Ferrari in the morning is always just like the first time ever," said *Car and Driver* in their rapturous road test of Ferrari's new 3.3-liter spyder in 1965. The nineteen-year-old Colombo V-12 had been stretched again. It still carried the SOHC heads and the standard, triple Weber carburetors. The dual-purpose, 3.3-liter GTB had been introduced with 280 hp. The GTS was detuned to 260 hp at 7000 rpm in deference to its more luxurious character. That does not imply the absence of the typical Ferrari's function. With the newly-enlarged engine came even more radical departures from traditional Ferrari road car practice. The five-speed, all indirect gearbox, first used in the racing cars, was fitted in unit with the differential. Four-wheel, independent suspension with fabricated, parallel wishbones was also introduced on the series, all within the well-proven 2400 mm wheelbase. Magnesium alloy wheels were standard, but more romantic fourteen-inch wire wheels were optional on both cars and they mounted fat, 205-sized tires. Top speed for the spyder was 144 mph, with 0-60 times of six seconds available in the rather heavy 3,318-pound machine. It still managed a respectable 15 mpg on the highway. Pininfarina designed and built two hundred examples of the new generation spyder. They were available for $14,500 in 1965. Not inexpensive until you consider their present value is twice that.

250 GT Lusso 1962-1964

275 GTS 1964-1966

Jerry Titus was a musician, engineer, technical editor of *Sports Car Graphic*, and a respected race driver. In his test of the "sober," luxurious air-conditioned 330 GTC, he described the cornering power thus: "The curve-warning speeds in Nevada are pretty realistic and generally can only be exceeded by 20 mph or so in a good vehicle. We stopped the speedo-reading when the Ferrari went through a '35-mph' corner at 95 and still wasn't very hung out!" Based on the chassis of the 275 GTB (front engine, rear gearbox), but with a four-liter, SOHC V-12 and 300 hp, the GTC was meant for *fast* touring. It retained the five-speed gearbox with the shift gate, the three big Weber carburetors, full independent suspension, four giant disc brakes and Ferrari's established 2400 mm wheelbase. The road performance was not far removed from the dual-purpose berlinetta, but at 3,100 pounds its destiny was unmistakable. Most of the examples imported to the West Coast even included air conditioning. As the car became available to road testers the phrase "finest all-round road Ferrari ever" became the standard description of the chunky coupe. It lived up to its reputation. At $14,900 it was also the most expensive production Ferrari ever (the super-expensive Superamericas were not for "production"). The factory claimed 165 mph for the GTC and contemporary tests put 0-60 times at a bit over seven seconds. Still a well-respected car among the cognocenti, its strong performance and ageless Pininfarina shape are maintaining its value in spite of its 10 to 15 mpg fuel consumption. Six hundred examples were produced by Pininfarina before the Daytona became "The Ferrari."

A curious anomaly exists in hand-formed cars. They are all imperfect. Not just a little. Not like Detroit's misaligned doors, but doors of two different sizes. The ends are not horizontal, they are frequently not even parallel. They are exquisitely inaccurate. The 275 GTBs are thus. They were $14,680, 166 mph, 0-60 in 6.2 seconds, GTO-inspired sculptures. The 3.3-liter V-12 was given four overhead cams. Six Weber carburetors, once reserved for racing, were present in their awesome glory. It all produced 300 hp at 8000 rpm. The race-bred, indirect, five-speed gearbox was hung in the rear. All racing car stuff, but that wasn't all. Fully independent suspension for each of the four wheels with parallel wishbones was also used. Fat 205x14 tires enhanced the fantasy. The voluptuous form was stretched over the customary 2400 mm wheelbase and it all weighed 2,663 pounds ready to do battle on Woodward Avenue. Scaglietti produced 280 GTB/4s after building 460 original two-cam GTBs to Pininfarina's design. A few GTBs found their way onto race tracks, but the 275 GTB/C was the factory race version and the GTB/4 had optional air conditioning just to establish its real purpose. Here was the consummate sensual machine. They even left out just enough insulation to let in the bite of the cacophony that is a Ferrari. It cannot be driven casually. It demands the attention of all your senses. Quick, agile, responsive, animal-like in its attachment to the root of your spine, it is the quintessential sports car.

330 GTC 1966-1968

275 GTB 4 1967-1968

Gloria Steinem notwithstanding, this is a man's car. Big, muscular, graceful in the manner of Nureyev, and brutally fast. It was introduced to the European market at the Paris Salon of 1968. Not until March of 1971 would the American Ferraristi be able to purchase a reinforced and detoxed example. While other exotic car manufacturers were extolling the virtues of mid-engined, racecar-like machines, Ferrari put his mighty 4.4-liter four-cam, six-carburetor, 352 hp V-12 in the front of his new 174-mph cafe racer. He did put the massive five-speed gearbox in the rear for balance, but the visual effect was an ancient concept in a modern shape. Though dubious at the outset, after a day with the car *Road & Track's* testers called it simply, "the best sports car in the world". It equalled the mid-engined exotics in almost every way, but was much more forgiving to the skilled amateur driver. The well-proven 2400 mm wheelbase now carried 3,600 pounds but 0-60 could still be done in 5.9 seconds. The parallel-wishbone, fully-independent suspension had been strengthened and refined. So effective was the combination that several enthusiastic owners began competing in the touring car category of the long distance races with some success. The factory eventually built fourteen racing cars called the 365 GTB/4A. Scaglietti built 1,300 Daytonas to Pininfarina's timeless design before the Boxer took its place. It originally sold for $19,500 in 1971. Most included air conditioning and, with detoxification, delivered 13 to 14 mpg. Nevertheless, it remains one of the most desirable Ferraris.

When a prototype alfresco Daytona was shown on the Pininfarina stand at the Paris Salon in 1969, phones began to ring at the factory in Modena. Production was simply not in Ferrari's plans. However, demand was high and Scaglietti seemed to be building more Daytonas than Ferrari could produce chassis. It was determined that they could slow Scaglietti and satisfy the demand by having the top cut off every fourth coupe until fifteen spyders were built. Five would go to Europe and five each would be sent to America's east and west coasts. These first cars were basically topless Daytona coupes. The 4.4-liter, DOHC, 352 hp V-12 still carried that marvelous row of six Weber carburetors. The rear-mounted, five-speed gearbox separated the independent rear suspension. The wheelbase and weight remained the same. The Daytona Spyder finally did go into a per-order production of about 125 cars, each selling for $25,500 in America. While the top speed remained 174 mph, for some reason the road test showed a 0-60 time of 6.7 seconds—0.8 seconds slower than the coupe. Scaglietti produced all the spyders, but a phenomenon occurred in the late seventies. The Daytona Spyder cult pushed the price up near $100,000 and a replica business exploded on the scene. You could buy a coupe for $30,000 and for an additional $15,000 you could have a car that looked exactly like the $90,000-plus real thing. By mid-1980 approximately fifty pseudo-spyders had been made around the world.

365 GTB 4 Daytona 1969-1974

365 GTS 4 Spyder 1971-1974

"A Ferrari for the mature enthusiast," said *Road & Track* in their July 1972 test. To establish the character of this luxurious car, one of their primary complaints was an ill-fitted bit of weather stripping which allowed wind noise to intrude on the passengers. In a Ferrari?! There was a time when *gear noise* drowned out wind noise in an *open* Ferrari. The GTC4 was introduced in Geneva in March of 1971 as the replacement for the 365 GTC and it took that gracious concept to new heights of refinement. To complement the luxurious new interior, the car had a very modern flat nose, a low hood, and the greenhouse was drawn in a graceful arc above the unadorned sweep of the side panels. The 4.4-liter V-12 was used, but there was a difference. A new series of heads had been cast with the intake ports between the intake and exhaust cams. Six side-draft Weber carburetors were suspended out over the fender wells to permit the extremely low hood. Though exotic looking indeed, the new configuration produced only 320 hp at 6200 rpm. At 3,800 pounds its only purpose was very comfortable, high-speed touring. It still managed 0-60 in 7.3 seconds and 152 mph. A smaller, front-mounted gearbox left room for small rear seats and the self-leveling, fully independent rear suspension maintained the ride. The handsome tourer was given a 2500 mm wheelbase to add space. At $27,500 it was the most costly Ferrari road car ever, but it did include air conditioning and a stereo/tape player. Pininfarina built five hundred GTC4s in three years.

Accolades flowed from the motoring press when the "little Ferrari" was introduced in 1967. It had a 2300 mm wheelbase, an all-aluminum body, an aluminum, two-liter, four-cam V-6 engine with 180 hp mounted transversely amidships, and a shape as exciting as an Italian mistress. It was named for Ferrari's son, who is credited with suggesting Ferrari build a V-6 engine. Two years passed before the new Dino was "federalized" for America. When it arrived it had gained 40 mm in wheelbase, a steel body, a cast-iron engine block, 400 cc of displacement, 15 hp, and about three hundred pounds. At 2,700 pounds its 0-60 acceleration was 7.9 seconds and fuel consumption had climbed to the 13 mpg range. However, it was still the most exciting shape available for road use. The engine had a legitimate claim to a couple of Ferrari world championships and that marvelous form bore a definite resemblance to recent Ferrari racing cars. Two additional years passed before the very popular spyder appeared. The steeply raked steering wheel, the joyously firm and positive five-speed gear change with its position gate, its busy, metallic drone that crept through the firewall all combined to prove its heredity. With fully independent suspension and enormous, ventilated disc brakes, the Dino was meant to be driven. It was stable at its highest attainable speed (about 144 mph) and its cornering power was highly praised in the contemporary press. By 1974 Scaglietti had produced 2,732 Dino GTs and 1,180 Spyders. In America they sold from $12,000 for a GT in 1970 to over $18,000 for a GTS in 1974.

365 GTC 4 1971-1974

246 GTS Dino 1972-1974

It seems incredible that in these homogenized, detoxified autumn years of the twentieth century you can purchase an automobile which can travel at greater speed than the fastest racing cars of only fifteen years ago. A Ferrari Boxer can not only consume three and a half miles in one minute, but you can converse in a normal voice and enjoy Verdi in air-conditioned opulence while doing so. The Boxer prototype was introduced at the Turin Show in 1971. It went into production in 1973 as the 365 GT/BB. The refined BB512 appeared late in 1976 with its 12-cylinder opposed (boxer) engine increased to a full five liters. The horsepower was actually reduced from 380 at 7500 rpm for the type 365 (the factory admits some exaggeration there) to a realistic 360 for the BB/512. Using current Ferrari race car technology, the Boxer has a large flat-twelve engine mounted amidships, but it is above its five-speed gearbox. The DOHC heads support four, three-throat, down-draft Weber carburetors. The 3,084 pound curb weight includes air conditioning, electric windows and stereo radio/tape deck. Interior space is quite generous, but the 2500 mm wheelbase and 4400 mm overall length allow little or no room for luggage. The performance figures of the two cars are identical, with 0-60 in six seconds and a top speed of 188 mph, but the mid-range power of the BB/512 makes it a much more pleasant car for daily use. Boxers are built by Scaglietti to a Pininfarina design and are available in Europe for the equivalent of $85,000. American conversions are an additional $30,000.

The first four-cam V-8 Ferrari, née Dino, was received with a great deal of skepticism. A Ferrari engine was a V-12. Even a V-6 was a Ferrari engine, but a V-8, even with four Webers, smacked of Fords and Chevys and — Fiats. Beyond the engine, the Bertone-styled 308 looked like an overweight Lamborghini, not a lithe, muscular classical Ferrari, but when the Pininfarina 308 GTB finally arrived it was joyously welcomed as the return of Ferrari and the salvation of the eighties. The four-cam V-8 was still there, transversely amidships, over its gearbox; but the car now looked like a Ferrari. In fact, it was all Ferrari. The new three-liter engine pumped out 225 hp at 7000 rpm — more than the old 250 V-12 did in its normal street tune. The wheelbase was 2300 mm, the same as the 246 Dino. Actually the American 308 equaled the 246 Dino in performance. It was more powerful, but 300 pounds heavier at 3,000 pounds. Early in 1978 the GTS was introduced. It was received with even more enthusiasm and has been an even greater sales success. With air conditioning and the ubiquitous stereo radio/tape deck standard, it sold for $34,195 on the East Coast and $36,411 in the West. By mid-1980 the price of the 3,300-pound spyder has escalated to $45,000 and still sales are active. A top speed of 151 mph and 0-60 time of 8.2 seconds are enjoyed in conversation if not in actual use. Fuel consumption in the 15-16 mpg range doesn't seem to deter the megadollar buyer. As of June 1980, 2,437 308 GTSs and 2,701 GTBs have been built.

BB 512 Boxer 1977-

308 GTS 1978-

What's in a Name?

The Ferrari name is shrouded in glory, surrounded by mystique, and mentioned with respect. Ferrari enthusiasts all have different reasons for their loyalty to the marque. One can look back on having seen the first Ferrari win at Silverstone in 1950. Another still remembers the sound of the legendary vee-twelves as they came screaming by the pits at Le Mans in 1957.

I was never that lucky. For me it began with a picture in a Swedish newspaper. I believe the year was 1956. Ingrid Bergman had been selected to receive that year's film prize at a gala ceremony in Stockholm. The picture showed the actress and her director-husband Roberto Rosselini arriving in the Swedish capital after a non-stop drive from Rome.

The elapsed time quoted in the caption translated into an incredible average speed. I could visualize the Ferrari negotiating curvy mountain roads in Northern Italy, hear the echo as the car roared through the long tunnels into Switzerland, and imagine it almost airborne as it traversed Germany on arrow-straight autobahns.

From then on the name Ferrari meant something special to me, and I could always recall the feeling by conjuring up the image of the satisfied look on Rosselini's face as he peeled off his perforated driving gloves with their cut-off fingers and grinned into the flashing cameras.

It would take more than two decades before I was able to increase my knowledge of Ferraris, before I had time to research the different models, and before I had the opportunity to drive them. Often, when you remove the nostalgia to uncover the naked truth, you find yourself disappointed. Not so with Ferraris — the more you know about them, the better they become.

The incredible performance of these machines, the beauty of their sculptured bodies, the glory of the victories — all is encapsuled in the name Ferrari. And these are the things I have attempted to recreate on the pages of this book — for my own enjoyment and yours.

Open spaces, free speed, no limits. It's all between the car, the road, and your own skill as a driver; and that's the way you want it to be when you are behind the wheel of a Ferrari. To the left, surrounded by golden California hills, Mike Cotsworth steers his Spyder California straight into the setting sun. Above, Bart McGrath guides his Spyder Dino through the sharp curve of a winding mountain road high above the Pacific Coast. To the right, John Dekker's brand new Boxer, precariously placed were it not for the unobstructed view across the endless Colorado prairie, tries its wings for the first time in freedom.

Presented to Enzo Ferrari by the parents of a World War One flying ace who was slain in the line of duty, the Prancing Horse was destined to reach worldwide recognition as a symbol of the ultimate sports car. Ferrari first used it for his racing stable, La Scuderia Ferrari; he placed the black stallion on a yellow shield, yellow being the official city color of his native Modena. In these photographs the Prancing Horse decorates, from left to right, a Daytona Coupe, a 275 Spyder, a 365 GTC4, and a 308 Spyder. The characteristic Ferrari script in the picture above right is found on the rear deck of the Boxer.

Glowing eyes in the twilight – eyes of an animal called the car. The eyes of a cat or a horse are vital to its function – but decorative as well. This is also the case with the headlights of a car. It was especially true when automotive design took its inspiration from the voluptuous, sensuous, streamlined forms of animals – remember the smooth shark noses, the toothy grins, and the aggressive nostrils? But even now, when computers have a hand in designing cars, the animal theme is visible – one can recognize a frog, a lizard . . . . Pictured from left to right are a 275 GTS, a 330 GTC, a 365 GTC4, a 275 GTB, and a 308 GTS.

Sumptuous elegance already characterized Ferrari's interiors in the early production models, as attested to by the above photograph of a 1960 Spyder California. The steering wheel, with its decorative horn button and engraved spokes, remained unchanged in the 275 GTB, right, and in the Lusso, farther right. The large photograph on the opposite page shows the interior of the 1971 365 GTC4, today still rivaling the 400 GT as the most civilized Ferrari. The new steering wheel is small and leather-covered. Below this picture, the top has been removed to show the intimate two-seater arrangement of the 308 Spyder.

Borrani wire wheels were standard on the early production cars, and available as an option on later models. Wires were used in racing as well, but with increased torque came the demand for stronger wheels. An alloy wheel was developed for racing and then introduced on the 1965 line of production models. A 1966 show car sported star-shaped wheels. This design was used on the race cars during the following year and then appeared on the Daytona when it was introduced in 1968. The same design is used on the Boxer, pictured on the left, as well as on the 365 GTC4. This model, however, still looks good with wires, as can be seen in the picture above. The Dino received its own design, pictured on the far left on this page.

Heart of a Ferrari – the engine. To the far right, the massive under-hood view of a 365 GTC4. A low profile required side-draft mounting of the six carburetors. Below it, the Ferrari script on the valve cover of a restored 250 engine. In its original form, it was not polished. Shown beside it, a Lusso engine with standard air cleaner. The decorative row of velocity stacks is the center of attention in the picture to the near right, featuring a Spyder California. The stacks were only used for racing, but their impressive look, as seen above on a SWB Berlinetta, makes them an irresistible option to the enthusiastic restorer.

Owner's pride takes on a humorous twist when furniture manufacturer Jim Hull puts on his Yellow Cab hat. Not that he needs any additional help in attracting passengers – his yellow 275 Spyder does it alone. To the right, Steve Gilman, behind the wheel of his Daytona, enjoys the reward of a successful entrepreneur. He wears a driving jacket of his own design, produced by his own automotive fashion organization – the Style Auto Company. The large photograph on the opposite page captures long-time Hollywood Ferrari dealer Chic Vandagriff. The early morning sun is showing above the edge of a Palm Springs mountain chain as he takes a pleasure drive in his 308 Spyder. Pictured below is Denver nightclub owner John Dekker warming up his brand new 512 Boxer for its maiden voyage.

A Chronology of Production

Enzo Ferrari has devoted his entire life to motor racing. That and his son have been his two great loves. Had his racing programs not required the additional revenue that production would bring, it is doubtful there would ever have been any Ferraris for the road.

The influences that trigger and direct genius are legion. For Ferrari they began with the "anvil chorus" from his father's metal fabricating shop below the room he shared with his brother. In lieu of engineering school he spent several years of apprenticeship with Fiat and Alfa Romeo, mastering the science of automobiles. During those formative years he made contact with the leaders in racing car design. He was given the opportunity to work with the innovative designer Vittorio Jano and his protegé Giocchino Colombo and the development wizard Luigi Bazzi. In the future, each would play a vital role in the saga of the Ferrari.

Early in 1930, when he was thirty-two, Ferrari formed a partnership in the northern Italian village of Modena for the purpose of selling and racing Alfa Romeo cars. It was called "La Scuderia Ferrari" (The Ferrari Stable). The young entrepreneur took a great stride into history when Alfa Romeo decided to end factory participation in racing and gave the entire team and its equipment to his fledgling firm.

Under Ferrari's leadership the team was nearly invincible in the mid-thirties. When the might of the Third Reich entered the scene, Scuderia Ferrari alone tried to compete. To assist in the struggle, Alfa sent Colombo to Modena to develop new twelve- and sixteen-cylinder machines in the scuderia's own shop.

In the summer of 1938, Alfa recalled the entire team to Milan, including its disgruntled leader. Ferrari, "the great agitator" and high priest of spontaneity, and Gobbato, director of Alfa Romeo and meticulous planner, shared only intolerance for one another. The inevitable clash

brought an end to Ferrari's twenty-year affiliation with Alfa.

The sales and service partnership of the scuderia was liquidated. With that capital Ferrari established a small manufacturing operaion in the scuderia building, which he owned. Wartime expansion and the government's recommendation of dispersement of industry caused him to construct a larger factory on a piece of land he owned near the village of Maranello. It was there he would create the racing car that would bear his name.

In 1946 Colombo was commissioned to draw up the engine for the new machine. He could not work quickly enough to suit Ferrari, so the services of a young draftsman named Aurelio Lampredi were secured. Many sound technical reasons supported the decision to build a V-12, not the least of which was Colombo's prewar experience with Alfa.

As Colombo spent less and less time in Maranello, Lampredi took on more and more responsibility. While the concepts of the all-alloy (single overhead-cam) V-12 are Colombo's, Lampredi and Development Chief Bazzi must be given credit for its refinement and ultimate success.

Until 1953 Ferrari's output of road cars was divided among small batches of V-12 types 166, 195, 212, 250, 340, 342 and 375. The "type" numbers represent the displacement of one cylinder in cubic centimeters. The under-three-liter V-12s were based on the original Colombo block dimensions. The three-liter and larger displacement engines were based on a new "long engine" designed by Lampredi. It was similar in concept and in many details to the earlier style SOHC V-12.

During its years of automobile construction, the foundry and machine shop of Ferrari have manufactured all the casting or forgings required for the engine blocks, heads, transmissions, differentials, suspension components, etc. Like most manufacturers, electrical parts, shock absorbers and such were purchased from the best firms available. Chassis frames have always been produced by small firms near the factory. In the early days, complete, driveable chassis were shipped to carrozzerias (coach building shops) to be clothed in the latest fashions. Later the chassis/body combinations were assembled and trimmed then sent to the factory for the installation of the drive train.

Several different small carrozzerias built the bodies, but the most representative examples of "the look" were from Pinin Farina, whose firm became the exclusive designer of Ferrari road cars about 1953. Heavily involved in mass production for Alfa Romeo, Fiat and Lancia, Pinin Farina opted to design and produce only

Enzo Ferrari, to the right, on a rare occasion photographed behind the wheel of one of his creations. The picture dates back to the early fifties (Interfoto, courtesy Road & Track). The photograph above captures the massive strength of Mr. Ferrari as, stripped down to shirt sleeves and suspenders, he prepares for action (Gunther Molter, courtesy Road & Track). Photographer Henry Wolf recalls having to wait most of the day before permitted five minutes of Mr. Ferrari's time. Mr. Wolf asked him to think about his new racing engine, and "Il Commendatore" took this now-famous pose. The portrait is from the mid-sixties.

the prototypes until the sales volume was sufficient to use the production line. Generally, the very limited production was left to the small shops of Mario Boano, who produced road cars, and Franco Scaglietti, who became associated with Ferrari through race car construction.

The **250 Europa**, introduced in 1954, was the first luxury production Ferrari. Twenty were built on a 2800 mm wheelbase with the long-block engines. Another thirty-five, produced during 1956 with a 2600 mm wheelbase, were designated the **Europa GT** and used a new 250 engine based on the Colombo block. This engine was destined to become the basis for much of Ferrari's competition success, as well as all production engines during the next decade.

The Europa GT was followed in 1955 by the **250 GT**, which was singularly responsible for making Ferrari a household word. At least eleven body styles were built on two different wheelbases. They were all called 250 GT but the Ferrari cult has attached its own nicknames in order to distinguish one from the other.

The first series had a 2600 mm wheelbase and the early models were thinly-disguised racing cars. Only a few were built. Two production coupes were introduced at Geneva in 1956, a berlinetta (a dual-purpose coupe used for touring or racing) and a luxury touring car with only fast, comfortable touring as its purpose. Scaglietti built seventy-three examples of the berlinetta during the next four years. They would bring Ferrari the World Championship for GT cars. It would come to be know as the **250 GT Tour de France** after its first overall win in that famous event. Boano built over 120 copies of the luxury model to a handsome Pinin Farina design. It is now known as the **250 GT Boano**.

In the midst of the 250 GT production, Ferrari introduced a new series at the Brussels Show in 1956. Conceived as exclusive transportation for the very rich, it was known as the **410 SA** (for Superamerica). Only sixteen were built by Pinin Farina to special order over the next four years.

A new and elegant line was developing at Pinin Farina. Its first offspring was a luxurious and rakish roadster, introduced at Geneva in 1957. It enjoyed a brief success as the **250 GT Pinin Farina Spyder**. Only forty-seven were built.

Ferrari production was beginning to develop rapidly by the close of the decade. Racing success was bringing production success.

The summer of 1958 saw the introduction of two important new Ferrari models. The first was an open version of the successful berlinetta. At the suggestion of Richie Ginther and West Coast dealer John von

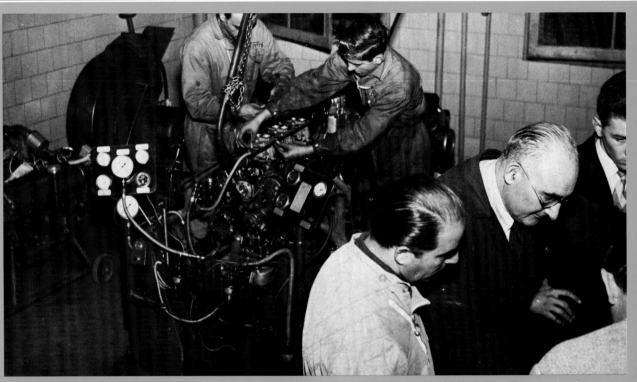

Unique interior photographs from the Ferrari factory, dated 1952. The view above shows an engine testing room with its center piece, the dynamometer. Luigi Bazzi, the long-time friend and collaborator of Enzo Ferrari and the man responsible for engine development, is seen surrounded by associates. Notice the single-carburetor engine resting on a stand along the wall. In the photograph to the left, a brake drum is being manufactured. The picture above right shows the assembly area for frame and suspension. Note the more complete chassis in the background and the gas tank to the left (Publifoto, courtesy **Road & Track**). The photograph to the right was taken in the factory courtyard at approximately the same time as the interiors. The rolling chassis, in this picture probably a 375 Mille Miglia, was tested this way and then driven to the coach builder for completion (courtesy Hilary Raab).

Neumann, American distributor Luigi Chinetti proposed the construciton of a dual-purpose roadster. It was called the **250 California** and Scaglietti made fifty on the 2600 mm wheelbase. The other was a very luxurious coupe, quite understated and formal in its styling. Though a very effective road car, it remains underrated by the serious Ferraristi. It has become known as the **250 GT Pininfarina Coupe**. Pininfarina (the new name in 1958) made over 350 of these lovely cars.

The fall of 1958 was spent testing and developing a successor to the remarkable Tour de France Berlinetta. The Paris Salon of 1959 hosted the introduction of the new berlinetta as well as an all-new car. To distinguish the California from the Pininfarina Spyder, a new **250 GT Cabriolet** based on the more sober lines of the Pininfarina Coupe went into production. By 1962 two hundred had been produced. The big news was the berlinetta. It was made more effective by shortening the wheelbase by 200 mm, at once making the 250 GT both lighter and more agile. The dual-purpose coupe became a legend as the **250 SWB** or **Short Wheelbase Berlinetta**. Scaglietti produced 166 bodies to Pininfarina's design. An additional fifty Californias were made on the new short wheelbase and renamed the **250 Granturismo Spyder California**.

At Le Mans in 1960, Ferrari unveiled its new family sedan. The **250 GT 2+2** or **GTE** was built on the 2600 mm wheelbase chassis with the engine moved forward by having new motor mounts cast into the block. Pininfarina made one thousand units, the last fifty of which had the bores increased to bring the capacity up to four liters. These few cars were called **330 Americas**.

Using a shortened **410 SA** chassis, Pininfarina began to experiment with automotive aerodynamics and aesthetics in 1956. The **Superfast I** was the result. Pininfarina had **Superfast II** built on a still shorter chassis in 1960 for his own use. It carried the concept into a new, modern direction. The introduction of the **400 Superamerica** at the 1960 Geneva Show put the Superfast shape into limited production. Pininfarina produced forty-eight examples. Further development produced a vast expanse of glass on the **400 Superamerica Superfast III** in 1962. The final statement in the series, **Superfast IV**, had four exposed headlights and was the least successful. The culmination of these studies was the **500 Superfast** of 1964. It combined the best of all the previous studies in a large, handsome form. Pininfarina built thirty-six of them.

The Paris Salon of 1962 was Pininfarina's choice for the introduction of his most elegant production shape. Combining the results of aerodynamic studies and traditionally conservative taste, Pininfarina excelled in the beautiful **250 GT Berlinetta Lusso**, built on the short wheelbase chassis. Scaglietti produced 350 during two years.

An interesting change occurred at this time. Prior to the Lusso, all Scaglietti bodies were hand-hammered, in either aluminum or steel, to line of sight. It wasn't until midway throught the Lusso production that a wooden buck was used to assure a consistent form for the bodies.

Concurrent with the Lusso was a new, larger 2+2. It would now seat four adults in comfort. In order to maintain Ferrari's reputation for the fastest road cars, a further increase in the capacity of the 1.5-liter Colombo V-12 took it to four liters. The new car was known as the **330 GT**. Its four-headlight nose did not set well with the customers, so a revised two-headlight arrangement was introduced along with a full five-speed gearbox to replace the four-speed-plus-overdrive of the first version. Power steering and air conditioning were offered as options for the first time on the renamed **330 GT 2+2**. A total of 1,085 were built by Pininfarina.

The 250 GT had run its course. Market pressure forced innovation. A five-speed gearbox and fully independent suspension were now *de rigeur* in a modern exotic car. The venerable, parallel-tube frame was redesigned to locate the big, race-proven, five-speed gearbox in unit with the differential. Fully independent rear suspension was included in the transformation, and a new era Ferrari was born. The incredible Colombo V-12 had its bores changed again, bringing the individual cylinder capacity to 275 cc and making the engine displacement 3.3 liters. Pininfarina created a form both modern and traditional that said Ferrari without question. The introduction was made at Paris' popular Salon in October of 1964 as the **275 GTB**. Scaglietti made 460 examples.

Sharing the debut of the GTB was the more conservatively drawn spyder, known as the **275 GTS**. Only two hundred of these handsome cars came from Pininfarina.

Inherent high-speed instability demanded a redesign in the GTB. A longer, lower nose was added in 1966, along with a worm and sector steering box which replaced the overly sensitive rack and pinion. The driveshaft was enclosed in a tube for the revised model. The open driveshaft with a center bearing had proved unreliable in the berlinetta but was retained in the spyder.

Approximately six months after the introduction of the 275 GTS, Ferrari offered another variation on the same

Pictured here are limited-production Ferraris and one-offs showing the styling development leading up to the first full-scale production models offered for 1959. Viewed clockwise: the 1953 250 Europa, the one-off 1955 375 America Cabriolet for ex-king Leopold, the 1956 Europa GT, the 1956 250 GT, directly influencing the limited-production 1957 Boano, the almost identical 1958 Ellena, the 1957 410 Super America, the one-off 1957 250 GT Spyder for race driver Peter Collins, and the 1958 410 Super America. (Photographs by Pininfarina, Rob de la Rive Box, Publifoto, Bernard Cahier, courtesy Hilary Raab and Road & Track).

theme. Using the 275 chassis, he installed the big four-liter engine and Pininfarina drew up a very conservative, luxury coupe. The **330 GTC** was a powerful and popular road car. A convertible model, the **330 GTS**, based on the body of the GTC, soon followed. Pininfarina built six hundred of the coupes and one hundred of the spyders.

As a replacement for the 500 Superfast, Pininfarina built fourteen enormous convertibles on the 330 GT 2+2 chassis and installed 4.4-liter engines. They were the **365 Californias**.

With the production touring cars now at four liters and 300 hp, an improved, dual-purpose berlinetta was needed. The **275 GTB/4** made its debut at the Paris Salon in the fall of 1966. It was the first production Ferrari with four overhead-cams and six carburetors. Its power output now matched the four-liter touring cars and, with the marvelous 275 GTB body it still carried, it weighed only 2,663 pounds. Scaglietti's craftsmen hand-formed 280 copies. Another request from Luigi Chinetti for an open car resulted in the construction of ten **275 GTS/4 NART Spyders**.

The enormous success of the new cars forced the doubling of the production facility at Maranello. Though the stresses of manufacturing continued to dissipate his energy, racing remained Ferrari's primary interest. The 1965 Formula Two rules, requiring engines built in minimum quantities of five hundred, had brought a veteran engine back to life. Franco Rocchi, who had joined Ferrari under Lampredi in 1949, redesigned the four-cam Dino V-6 so it could be mass produced by Fiat. In 1967, after the Fiat Dinos were well into production, the Ferrari design staff developed a Dino of its own. It used the same Fiat-produced, two-liter V-6, but mounted it transversely amidships, ahead of a new five-speed gearbox. Only 150 aluminum-bodied **Dino 206 GTs** were produced. Scaglietti built the bodies to a Pininfarina design.

By 1968 Ferrari found himself in a pitched battle with his old customer Lamborghini for the world's fastest road car. Though having successfully built mid-engined racing cars for some time, Ferrari was not yet willing to give up the forgiving handling of the front-engine, rear-gearbox design developed in the 275/330 series. Rocchi's staff designed twin-overhead-cam heads for the big, 4.4-liter engine originally developed for customer racing cars only three years before. Six twin-choke Weber carburetors were mounted and an output of 352 hp was the result. The sweeping shape which Pininfarina designed was again produced in the shops of Scaglietti. It was called the "Daytona" by the European press in honor of Ferrari's win at that race in

January of 1967. There were 1,300 **365 GTB/4 Daytonas** built between 1968 and 1973. From 1972 to 1973 125 **Daytona Spyders** were built as well, but only on a special-order basis.

A new, even larger 2+2 was introduced in 1968 which used the big 4.4-liter engine but with single-overhead-cams and three Weber carburetors. It also incorporated the front-mounted gearbox of the 330 GT 2+2. Pininfarina built 801 examples of the **365 GT 2+2** during its three years of production.

The 4.4-liter engine was used again in the 330 series coupe and spyder. The resulting models were called the **365 GTC** (150 were built) and the **365 GTS** (only twenty were built).

The ever-increasing demands of the production side of his company caused Ferrari to take a closer look at his affiliation with Fiat. An agreement was reached in 1969 which gave Fiat control of all Ferrari production, but left Enzo Ferrari with final approval on any new product and control of all racing. Guiseppe Dondo and Francesco Bellicardi moved to Maranello from Torino, and another era began. In order to isolate themselves from the increased activity at the factory, Franco Rocchi, Angelo Bellei, and Giorgio Salvarani, all twenty-year veterans of Ferrari design, moved their technical staff of twenty men to Modena and a sparkling new facility.

The first product of the new arrangement was a revised Dino. The four-cam V-6 was redesigned with a cast-iron block and increased to 2400 cc. The wheelbase was up two inches and Scaglietti now made the bodies of steel. The **246 GT** was duplicated 2,732 times between 1970 and 1974. An alfresco model called the **246 GTS** was introduced in 1972 and 1,180 were produced in the next two years.

The 365 GTC, the body of which dated back to 1965, was beginning to look a bit long of tooth. It was replaced by an even more luxurious tourer called the **365 GTC4**. More than a simple revision, it was a totally new car. Its most innovative departure from traditional Ferrari practice was the new head design. In order to permit a lower hood line, the intake ports were placed between the camshafts and six Weber side-draft carburetors were placed horizontally away from the engine center line. A new, smaller five-speed gearbox was mounted immediately behind the flywheel/clutch assembly and the self-leveling, fully independent rear suspension of the 365 GT 2+2 was used. A very rakish new body was designed and built by Pininfarina. It survived for only two years and a production run of five hundred.

In 1972 a totally new 2+2 was introduced. It included most of the mechanical innovation of the GTC4, but had

Pinin, Ferrari's first four-door, was introduced by Pininfarina in the spring of 1980. The classic rounded forms conceal the powerful Boxer engine mounted up front. To the left, the rear end treatment of the Pinin, and to the right, its elegant lines from a three-quarter angle. The frontal styling returns to the upright grill of early Ferraris. At the point of writing, eventual production plans have not been disclosed. The remaining photographs show the Mondial – a two-door four-seater, introduced in Europe in 1979, but not available in the United States until the summer of 1981. Pininfarina's styling shows the heritage of both the 308 GTB and the Boxer (Pininfarina, courtesy Giancarlo Perini).

an extended wheelbase to accommodate four adults in its leather-lined interior. Pininfarina built 524 of the **365 GT4s** before the engine was increased to five liters and a GM automatic transmission was added to create the **400 Automatic**. By the summer of 1980 550 have been produced; of those about thirty percent have had the optional five-speed manual transmission.

The Dino prospered during the fuel-conscious seventies, but production costs continued to drive the retail price up as America's emission laws drove the performance down. An all-new three-liter V-8 was designed by Rocchi's team to power Ferrari's new export car. It was first available as the **308 GT4**, a popular and practical, four-place car designed by Bertone and introduced at the Paris Salon in October 1973. In 1977 a two-liter V-8 version was introduced as the **208 GT4**. Now out of production, Bertone manufactured 2,850 three-liters and 700 two-liters by 1980.

In 1974 the eagerly-awaited two-place coupe was available for tests. The **308 GTB** was delightful. Bob Bondurant called it "the best sports car I've ever driven." Both the GTB and the **308 GTS** that followed were designed by Pininfarina and built at Scaglietti. They are the first Scaglietti-built bodies formed by electric-power hammers rather than human-power hammers. As this is written, there have been 2,701 GTBs, 1,100 of which were in fiberglass, and 2,437 GTSs manufactured.

The *piece de résistance* of the Fiat-controlled production was certainly the device first shown to the public at the 1971 Paris Salon. Though an enormous visual success, it was not approved for production until late in 1973. The *Reparto Industrial*, the official name of the production arm of Ferrari, took on a truly monumental task: a flat (boxer) twelve with 380 enthusiastic cavalini mounted amidships over its five-speed gearbox. A delicious new and modern form to surround all the machinery and two fortunate humans. It was called the **365 GT/BB**. It might have been the Ferrari magic carried to its ultimate conclusion, but for one thing. It was replaced after Scaglietti had built only 387 by an even more awesome machine. The **BB512** was the same car more finely tuned. Scaglietti has built about 550 of the improved car by 1980.

As this is written the next generation 308, the four seater **Mondial,** has just been introduced and Ferrari's first four-door has been seen at selected auto shows. Named **Pinin,** it is a tribute to the maestro whose name it bears. It is elegant in an aggressive way. The great boxer twelve resides under its expansive hood and an opulent, electronic, leather-lined compartment invites human occupation. It may be the last of the great twelves.

250 GT CALIFORNIA

Of Cops and Canvas Ripping

I have always known that some facts are more intriguing than others. I mean facts like these.

During the summer of 1959, a certain Bill Helburn decided to purchase a new Ferrari 250 GT Spyder California. He placed his order with the Chinetti dealership in New York, who in turn passed it on to the Ferrari factory in Modena.

The California was completed during the early part of 1960. Onto the identification plate on the fire wall was stamped: 508 D/1641 GT. Onto the engine block, on the flywheel housing: 1641 GT. And onto one of the timing chain covers: 168.

What intrigued me was that now, twenty years later, after the California had spent its first decade in relative obscurity, and its second in total obscurity — symbolically hidden under a tree — it was still possible to place the car in its historical space just by researching some letters and numerals. It was not just a beautiful sculpture of cast iron and aluminum with an anonymous past. No, it had roots, and they could be traced!

The number 508, for instance, referred to the type of chassis used and meant that the car was built on the 2600 mm long-wheelbase frame. The letter D indicated that the chassis was in its last stage of development, just before it was changed to the short-wheelbase configuration, type 536. 1641 was the individual chassis number, and a closer look at the factory records revealed that it was the fifth from the end of the long-wheelbase production run.

So far so good! The numbers made sense, except for the number found on the timing chain cover — 168. It

The two pictures on the right-hand page show a Pinin Farina Spyder, chassis number 0789. A forerunner to the Spyder California, it is often mistaken for the latter. A noticeable difference is the crease along the side of the body; another is the high location of the taillights. At the top of this page, the dashboard and engine of the Pinin Farina Spyder. Above, a photograph from the Ferrari factory, labeled "chassis of the new California." To the left, a short-wheelbase, open-headlight Spyder California. (All photos by de la Rive Box, courtesy the Hilary Raab Collection, except the Factory shot by Bernard Cahier, courtesy Road & Track.)

was confusing, since long-wheelbase Californias were normally fitted with type 128 engines. Type 168 seemed wrong for the car. But engine and chassis numbers corresponded, which indicated that the car still had its original engine. Something unusual had happened here!

That is what I mean. Some facts are more intriguing than others.

When Mike Cotsworth first found out about 1641, he had been searching for an open Ferrari for some time. He had looked at the Pininfarina Cabriolet, but had realized it was unsuitable for racing, and he wanted a car he could race. He knew about the California, and how few had been made, but he had never seen one. And if by chance one would have come up for sale, he knew he would never have been able to afford it!

In 1978, while attending the Historic Races in Monterey, to his surprise he discovered a California parked in the paddock. While he was taking a closer look, a man dressed like a cowboy walked up next to him.

"I have a car like this, but mine is aluminum," the man said.

They talked about it for awhile. The man said he had not driven his car for the past seven years. He also seemed willing to sell it if the price was right.

A few days later, Mike and his wife, Vicki, went to see the car. A four-hour drive south along the Pacific Coast brought them to its hiding place. As soon as Mike saw it sitting under the tree, he knew he wanted no part of it!

The car was covered with straw and dust and wrapped in cobwebs. The seats were torn and rotting. The wood-rimmed steering wheel was faded and cracked. The plexiglas headlight covers were broken and had been hidden in the trunk. To top it off, there were dark spots on the paint from the acidic berries that had fallen from the tree over the past seven summers.

The car was cleaned off with a broom and started. It was a wonder that it ran. The timing was off, and when they took it for a test drive it sounded more like a lawn mower than a sports car!

Afterward, Mike took Vicki by the arm and told the owner they were going for a short walk. As soon as they were beyond hearing range, Vicki started talking, with excitement written all over her face.

"Mike! Do you see what it can look like? All it needs is a real clean-up! Well, the seats have to be redone. But we can fix the steering wheel ourselves. And I know you can do the engine. It might not need much work at all. Did you see that it had gone only 40,000 miles? Aren't

(continued on overleaf)

pyder Californias were dual-purpose cars. You could drive them to the track, race them with success, then drive them back home again. But only a few Californias, such as the example photographed here, were actually built by the Factory specifically for racing. Under the skin of original paint, the body is all aluminum; the quick-release filler cap leads to an oversized gas tank; the engine is hot, delivering considerably more power than the normal Californias. This car is the fifth from the end of the Long Wheelbase production run. The chassis number is 1641, and it was completed in January of 1960. In spite of the fragile body, present owner Mike Cotsworth drives his California to the limit in vintage racing events. Before ending up in Mike's hands, the car had been sitting idle under a tree for seven years, losing all traces of its previous history. It's about time the car sees some action, reasons Mike. After all, that is what it was built for!

you pleased?"

Mike was startled. He had been sure Vicki felt the same way he did. Now he stopped abruptly . . . looked at her . . . then at the California. And suddenly he too saw it! They walked back to the owner.

"Well. We have a deal!" Mike said and reached for his checkbook. He still knew he could not afford it.

"Swell!" The owner looked relieved. "The Ferrari was too much for me. Always liked my Corvette better!"

The next day, Vicki got a loan from her Credit Union.

The red Ferrari sat quiet on the dark pavement of Zinfandel Lane. The day was coming to an end, and the budding green of the vineyards slowly turned orange as the sun set over Napa Valley.

I opened the door and let my body slide down along the back of the seat. As I sank down in the leather, my eyes eagerly recorded the view of the classic Ferrari steering wheel, the two large dials behind it, the black crackle-finish dash; beyond the windshield was the vast red surface of the long hood with its protruding air scoop in the center and the two sweeping fenders on each side.

"You race it at vintage events, I know, but did the first owner race it too?" I asked Mike as he sat down in the passenger seat.

"I believe he must have," said Mike, "because the car is definitely set up for racing. It has an all-aluminum body, a Tipo 168 engine, the 130 cam shafts with a 10 mm lift, and very wild timing. It has the ribbed, lightweight gearbox; it has an oversized gas tank with an external filler cap, and four-wheel disc brakes! It was all done at the factory. I have a copy of the factory assembly sheet showing it."

I turned the ignition key. The ticking sound of the fuel pump reached me from behind. After a few seconds its rhythm slowed down, indicating that the carburetors were filled. I pushed the key. And there it was — the legendary canvas-ripping roar of the Ferrari vee-twelve at my command!

I lowered my hand to the gear-shift lever and pushed it forward. There was some resistance at first. I applied more pressure; it was immediately pulled into place. I soon realized there was not much need for first gear. Quickly into second! Now I really felt the acceleration. Into third! The end of Zinfandel Lane came up on me abruptly. I turned right on Highway 29 and accelerated again. There was too much traffic on 29, so I turned left at Oakville and cut over to Silverado Trail, crossed it, and went up Howell Mountain Road. The next few miles were filled with beautiful curves as we climbed higher

Pictured on the left-hand page, the Pininfarina Cabriolet in three different appearances: top up, top down, and with optional hardtop. The pictures on this page feature the classic lines of the Pininfarina Coupe. Both of these models were too conservatively styled to be well-received at the time. Today, they are experiencing a well-deserved re-evaluation. Above, a Pininfarina styling-rendering, which, if produced, would have given the Coupe a sportier look. Notice the low greenhouse and the hood scoop. To the right, the elegant interior of the Coupe. (All photos by Pininfarina, courtesy the Hilary Raab Collection.)

and higher up the steep hill.

The ride was stiff but not uncomfortable. There was some play in the steering wheel: I had a hard time getting used to it. I felt a slight understeer as well. The car had a tendency to roll a little in the corners, and the back end jumped a few times. But my overall impression was one of surprise at how easily the car could be controlled. Everything was lighter than expected — the steering, the shifting, the clutching. Everything but the brakes. Mike warned me repeatedly about them as we turned and went down the hill, returning to St. Helena.

We crossed Silverado Trail again and were safely down in the valley. I practiced shifting on the short straightaway back to the highway.

Leaving the stop sign and turning left in front of Christian Brothers Winery, I noticed a black-and-white. The policeman stared longingly at the Ferrari as he passed in front of us. I knew what he wanted, so I gave it all I had, accelerating up between the long rows of century-old moss-covered trees. I passed the cop right in front of Beringer Winery, doing over ninety. I caught a glimpse of him as he flung himself back against the seat, counteracting his kick on the gas pedal. But nothing helped — he was standing still! I watched in the rear-view mirror as the black-and-white was reduced to a dark spot in the distance.

Of course, it was all in my imagination. But I felt good just fantasizing about it. I kept my thirty miles per hour, patiently trailing the police car until I reached Zinfandel Lane again. I turned left on it, continued up to the end of the road and switched off the engine. The sun was now completely obscured behind the hills to the west. I knew this was the quiet time of the day — except in my ears, where the lovely canvas-ripping sound remained. I listened to it for awhile.

Mike finally turned to me. "I don't think I told you this before," he said. "There is an interesting diagram in the factory assembly sheet. It shows the results of the dynamometer testing of the engine. During the first session, they recorded a power output of 256 hp; this was done at 7000 rpm. Then — and this is the significant thing — they made another test, this time at 7500 rpm. Now they recorded 272 hp!

"Well, that definitely proves that it had the 168 engine all along. The standard engine could never have performed that well!

"It also means that my California is one of the few competition versions left with the original engine still in it!"

Like I said, some facts are just more intriguing than others.

250 GT SWB

Dual Purpose Dilemma

The weather was still beautiful when an announcement suddenly came crackling over the speaker. A hailstorm was on its way.

I looked around and saw expressions of surprise and disappointment. There were over 100 Ferraris at the Road America race course. It was the annual gathering for members of the Ferrari Club of America. I could imagine what hail would do to those polished surfaces.

I looked to the west. There was a mass of dark clouds hanging on the horizon. I looked up. The sky was still blue here over Elkhart Lake.

Suddenly, as if on command, all heads turned in the direction of a savage sound like that of thunder. But it had nothing to do with the approaching storm. In fact, the hail was forgotten while all eyes concentrated on the swarm of Ferraris accelerating up the straightaway toward the pit area.

First in view was a 312 T3 Formula One car. With its 12,000-rpm capability, its high-pitched scream almost shattered my ear drums. The 312 was chased by a 512 Le Mans Boxer, equally inconsiderate, except that now the damage was done by a deep, metallic roar.

Then came the sound I had been waiting for — that of the classic vee-twelve engine eagerly working itself up to top revs, increasing in ferocity as it approached, nostalgically melodious as it passed. It was hard-charging Chuck Reid in his 1961 Short Wheelbase Berlinetta. He shifted to fourth just in front of the pit. The nose of the car dipped for a moment as Chuck let up on the accelerator, then it changed angle again, the rear squatting deep, the

Photographed before its participation in the 1959 Le Mans race, the Interim Berlinetta prototype stands ready for action. (Photo by Pininfarina.) Below it, a 1960 competition SWB Berlinetta. Note the sliding plexiglas windows with ventilation holes. The row of interior pictures shows the variation in dashboard layouts. From left to right: an Interim Berlinetta, a competition version, and a 1962 steel-bodied car. (Photos by de la Rive Box, except far right by Dean Bachelor.) Pictured on the upper right, Stirling Moss at speed in the 1961 Nassau Tourist Trophy Race. (Photo by Action Ltd., courtesy Road & Track.)

nose pointing high, as he opened up the throttle and let the 265 wild horses dig in with full power.

Chuck's mechanic, Windy Foreman, was standing beside me. We both followed the dark blue Berlinetta intently with our eyes until it disappeared over the top of the hill, shooting down toward Turn One. There was a faint trail of blue smoke behind the right pair of exhaust pipes.

"Do you think it means trouble?" I shouted to Windy, trying to make myself heard over the noise of a passing Testa Rossa.

"Probably not. But you never know!"

In the good old days of sports car racing, most cars were of dual-purpose character. This meant that you could drive the car to the track, compete successfully with it after a minimum of changes and afterward, with passenger, luggage and trophy in place, drive it back home again. The fastest production sports cars of today are too much on the road but not enough on the track. The Short Wheelbase Berlinetta was the ultimate dual-purpose car; it was nimble and flexible in traffic, yet fiercely competitive as a race car.

The SWB was based on the successful competition berlinetta of the mid- and late fifties. A new berlinetta, still built on the long-wheelbase chassis but clearly showing the new styling, made its debut at Le Mans in 1959. It is referred to as the Interim Berlinetta. In the Tour de France, the interim version took first overall. Only seven cars were made before the Short Wheelbase prototype was unveiled at the Paris Salon in the fall.

The SWB captured the four first places in the GT class at the 1960 Le Mans, and the three first overall positions in the Tour de France that year. The following year it took the four first overall places in the same event, and it again won the GT class at Le Mans. These were only some of the more prominent wins. In addition, there were innumerable victories in international, national and local events the world over. All this was accomplished with about 100 actively-raced cars out of 200 that were built.

Chuck Reid's SWB was still smoking as it came by on the next lap, although it seemed to be running beautifully. But on the third lap, as he rounded Turn Fourteen, instead of accelerating he raised his arm out the window, signaling that he was coming into the pit.

"What's wrong?"

Windy was immediately at the window, asking the question even before Chuck had pulled off his helmet.

(continued on overleaf)

Early Ferrari production models were thinly-disguised race cars, but never was it more evident than with the Short Wheelbase Berlinetta. If you had the money, you could buy a car like the one that won at Le Mans in 1960 and 1961. There were differences between them, notably in weight and tuning, but the car you drove on your Sunday morning excursions would for all practical purposes be identical to the famous Le Mans winner. Chuck Reid, owner of the 1961 chassis number 3087, photographed here by the Elkhart Lake race track, also owns another SWB. He keeps one in California for vintage racing, and another at his home in Texas. Can't live without them Berlinettas!

"Nothing serious! It just feels like the engine is running out of gas when I'm doing top revs in third. Could I be low on gas already?"

"Not a chance! You should have plenty left!"

"What about the fuel pump?"

Windy took Chuck's place in the driver's seat. He flicked on the switch operating the manual pump, but the clicking sound was not heard.

"It's not working!" he exclaimed.

Windy came out from behind the wheel and quickly squeezed under the car. Chuck was relaxed; easing up on the neckband of his driving suit, he turned to me.

"Why don't you put on a suit and a helmet? I've checked with the starter and you can go along as a passenger for two laps. This problem shouldn't take long; it's probably only a faulty connection."

I looked around. Dyke Ridgley happened to walk by just then; he seemed to be about my size. I must not have concealed my excitement very well, because I only had to say a few words before he began to strip. The suit was tight, but I managed to zip it up and press the helmet over my head without peeling off my ears. I was in my seat just as Windy gave us the go-ahead signal. We accelerated onto the track and reached Turn One just ahead of a Daytona.

Chuck kept it in third through Turn One, then accelerated, leaving it in third on the short straightaway up to Turn Three, where he prepared for the sharp curve by braking strongly and downshifting to second. He accelerated out of the turn, the car leaning low, and licked the marker on the left side of the track; he ran it up to 7400, shifted into third, ran it up to 7400 again, and shifted into fouth. We now had a long straightaway ahead of us, and I ventured a question.

"Do you always double-clutch?"

"Yes! You bet!" he replied emphatically. "You want to be as easy as you can on the clutch and the gearbox. I also listen to the sound of the engine to know when to shift, but it's best to look at the tachometer!"

"Next is a blind corner," he said, as we passed a bridge. We were coming up on Turn Six.

"You want to be in second before you reach the bridge. Then you want to tap the brake, like this. You want to tilt the balance of the car over to the right; that's very important!"

The corner went ninety degrees to the left, but I had no idea of that until we were already in it. Chuck shifted into third as we entered the Carousel. This was a long sweeping curve.

"You want to stay in the middle of the road here, giving the car more throttle as you advance, keeping the nose

The 1963 400 Superamerica, pictured at the left, is one of very few examples produced of this top-of-the-line 2+2 model. The smooth frontal area and the luxurious interior were distinctive features. At the other end of the spectrum was the 250 2+2, or GTE. Pininfarina's prototype is pictured at the top of this page. The dash was attractive and well-organized, above. Featured to the right is the rear quarter of the production version. Compare this view with the rare photograph, top left, of Pininfarina's scale model, specially-crafted for aerodynamic studies. (All photographs are by Pininfarina, courtesy the Hilary Raab Collection.)

pointing to the right, until almost to the end of the curve when you ease it over to the right, clipping the markers, and then you let it drift out to the left. Marvelous corner, isn't it! It's fantastic!"

He smiled as we came out of the curve with screaming tires. I didn't smile but I did agree with him. We were approaching Turn Eleven.

"I enjoy this one too! It separates the men from the boys. If you keep the correct line through it you don't have to let up at all!"

We swept around the last few curves and accelerated up the start-and-finish straightaway, completing one lap. For the first time I had a chance to look at the speedometer. We were doing 130.

After letting me off on the next pass, Chuck went out again. He wanted to put in as much driving time as possible. We saw him come by two more times, the car still running like a clock. The third time, he should have appeared between two Daytonas, but he did not show at all. Had he spun? Was he hurt?

Twenty minutes later the tow truck arrived with the SWB dangling lifelessly behind it.

"What happened?" Windy asked.

"There was a metallic sound in the engine coming out of the Carousel," Chuck said. "I pulled off immediately and killed it. I couldn't run it one more second. It sounds serious, I know that!"

Chuck was still behind the wheel. I sat down in the passenger seat. The sky was very dark now.

"That's all for today," he said with a sigh, and wiped off his forehead with the back of his hand.

"Depressing, isn't it?" I said. "The car breaks down and now we're getting a hailstorm too!"

"Yeah; it's depressing. I don't mind the storm, but now I can't drive the car back home to Houston. That bothers me!"

Chuck was quiet for a moment, then he said:

"Marvelous car though, isn't it? A true dual-purpose car. So flexible. So strong. Great car!"

We sat in silence for a long time, then Chuck broke the silence abruptly.

"Well, what the heck! Let's have a cigar!"

He reached across to the glove compartment, pulled out a box, opened the lid and invited me to take the first one. They were Joya de Nicaraguas.

"Contraband from Nicaragua," he smiled.

"Do you have a match?" I wondered.

"What do you need a match for? We'll use the cigarette lighter in the car. Here! I told you it was a true dual-purpose car!"

250 GT LUSSO

The Beauty and the Giant

Life is full of disappointments. One that many a Ferrari enthusiast is all too familiar with is the disappointment of not being able to afford what he wants. But it could be worse!

Imagine that you have picked out the Ferrari of your dreams. You have the money. You just want to try it out before you make the deal. But when you squeeze your body behind the wheel, you find that you don't fit. You are too tall!

Mister X, a Ferrari enthusiast from Saratoga, California, who prefers to remain anonymous, knows all about that kind of disappointment. He is six-foot-six!

Mister X had wanted a Ferrari ever since he first heard the sound of one at a race in Pebble Beach. The first model he tried out was a Pininfarina Coupe. He didn't fit. Then he tried an SWB. Again, he didn't fit. The one that finally gave him enough room was a 250 GTE 2 + 2, so he bought it. The car was white with a black leather interior, and he drove it to and from work every day.

Although he was quite satisfied with the 2 + 2, Mister X never felt it provided everything he expected from his dream car. He wanted something sportier! And he wanted a machine he knew to be the ultimate, one he could keep forever and always be satisfied with — mechanically, esthetically and historically.

The styling of the Lusso was already being praised when the prototype was first shown in the 1962 Paris Salon. The passing of time has confirmed it as one of Pininfarina's most outstanding Ferrari efforts. The rare photographs printed on these pages, showing interiors from Pininfarina's styling studio and Scaglietti's assembly line, have never before been published. On the clay model, above left, notice the lack of an air inlet on the hood. At this point it still only has a blister, much like that on the GTO, but more specifically rounded at the beginning. The picture to the right shows the crude state of the model, as if the final smoothing touches have not yet been added. The unique combination of blinker and bumper guard is already here, but the driving lights have not yet been removed from the grille. (Photographs courtesy the Hilary Raab Collection.) The other two pictures show the unpainted Lusso steel body, without and with running gear. The hood, doors and trunk lid were of aluminum. (Photographs courtesy of John Hajduk, Motorkraft, Bensenville, Illinois.)

Late in 1964, a certain gentleman from San Francisco took delivery of a Lusso at the Factory. The car had chassis number 5955, and was the last to roll off the production line — a fact no one seems to have taken special notice of at that time. He drove the Lusso in Italy for a while, on one occasion even showing it in a Concours d'Elegance at Montecatini. A picture of him with the car appears in the Ferrari Yearbook of 1964.

Later, he shipped the Lusso to San Francisco, where he drove it a total of about 5,000 miles. Then he left it with the local Ferrari dealer on Geary Street, who was also a Buick dealer, and stored it there for a long time. But one day it was gone.

At the time, no one knew why he had accepted the dealer's offer of a new Riviera and a new Skylark in an even trade for a Ferrari.

Meanwhile, Mister X had been promoted, and his travels occasionally took him to Italy. As expected, at first opportunity he visited the Ferrari factory. He was honored when the plant manager himself conducted the tour. At the conclusion of the tour, which happened to coincide with the end of the workday at the factory, they found themselves at the main gate. They were exchanging final niceties when suddenly, without warning, a door opened in the terra-cotta-colored building.

A group of men emerged, all very formal in dark business suits. They created a curiously comical picture as they filed out in the hot afternoon brightness. The unreal mood of the moment was amplified by the loud and relaxed conversation of the workers on their way home. It was a surprise when the last man to come out appeared without a jacket, his white shirt and suspenders creating a startling visual contrast to the dark suits. The tall and massive figure exuded unusual strength and self-confidence. It was "Il Commendatore" himself!

The plant manager excused himself and sprinted after Ferrari, who, during a brief exchange of words with the manager, glanced over his shoulder in the direction of the visitor. He then went back to the building reappearing a few moments later wearing a jacket. Adjusting his tie, and with the plant manager in tow, Ferrari smilingly approached Mister X, stretched out his arm and greeted the customer with a firm handshake.

"Mamma mia, cacaldo!" he exclaimed

"Very hot!" the plant manager translated.

"It's always a pleasure to talk with a customer. What do you own?" Ferrari continued.

"I have a 1961 2 + 2. I like it very much, although, I wish I had a Berlinetta. But all the models are very exotic

(continued on overleaf)

G raceful, elegant, refined – a few of the many superlatives used to describe the styling of the Lusso. In one word, it is referred to as the most beautiful of the Ferraris. Certainly Pininfarina's design, drawing inspiration from both the SWB Berlinetta and the LMB, is very seductive. From the aggressively-protruding front and the swelling fenders – stopping just short of becoming fat – to the smoothly-sinking curve of the roof, ending unexpectedly in the cut-off rear, it all translates into a powerful yet graceful sculpture of motion. The 1965 Lusso decorating these pages was photographed in the wooded hills above Saratoga, California. The chassis number is 5955 – the last of the Lussos!

and beautiful machines."

"Thank you. I build road cars so I can continue racing. Others race so they can sell the cars they build!" Ferrari said, and examined Mister X's six-foot-six frame.

"I have difficulty fitting behind the wheel, as you can see," Mister X explained.

"Perhaps we can build a car especially for you," Ferrari said with a smile, and then indicated with another handshake that the brief audience was over. He returned with energetic steps to the still-open door, and was again consumed by his own creation.

Mister X would always remember the occasion.

The Lusso that once belonged to the gentleman from San Francisco had been in the hands of Mister X for almost fifteen years when I met him. I arrived at his home in Saratoga around seven-thirty in the morning; we had agreed on meeting early so we could drive the Lusso up into the hills and photograph it there just as the morning fog disappeared.

"The sun will begin to burn it off in about an hour, I would say," Mister X told me as he came out in front of the house, where I was looking up at the hills. There was a heavy blanket of fog seeming to reach all the way up to San Francisco, totally enveloping the mountain chain.

"Well, let's look at the Lusso in the meantime." I suggested, as I caught a glimpse of its swelling fender forms in the darkness of the garage.

"It looks even better than when it was new!" I said. "I can see that it hasn't been restored. When a car is well-kept, over the years it acquires a patina. It becomes better than new!"

"Thank you! I'm happy that you, too, are of that opinion," replied Mister X. "Not everyone would agree with you, you know."

"When a car has been maintained like this, there's no question about it."

"Thanks! I have to tell you the story of how I got it. I went to a dealer one day, looking for parts for my 2+2. Just by chance, I became intrigued by some unfamiliar forms under a cover. When it was rolled back, revealing the Lusso, I really liked what I saw. When I sat in it and found that I fit, I knew it had to become mine. I felt like Enzo had fulfilled his promise and built a car for me!

"I told the dealer I had to have this car," Mister X continued. "He said it belonged to a customer, and that it wasn't for sale. But, I returned often and bugged him about it. Finally he said he would see what he could do. It's thanks to my persistence and his negotiating skill that I own it today!"

I sat down behind the wheel and was overcome with a

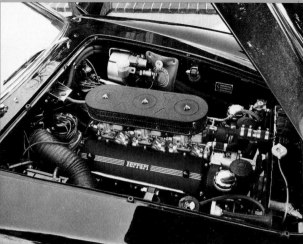

strong feeling of pleasure. This sensation was the result of three things: the spaciousness created by all the glass, especially by the large quarter windows; the rich elegance of that blue-gray leather, covering the seats as well as the entire luggage area behind them; and the enormous tachometer and speedometer, conspicuously placed in the center of the dashboard. The odometer showed 23,000 miles.

I stepped out and looked at "the most beautiful of the Ferraris" from all angles. I happened to notice that the knock-off wings were totally undamaged.

"How did you manage to keep them that way?" I asked Mister X.

He strode over to his workbench and returned with a curious-looking hammer.

"I make my own hammers, " he explained. "I use soft lead. Melt it myself on the stove and pour it into a small orange juice can. I had the model shop at work make this special handle for me."

"What about the hammer in the tool kit?" I asked.

"Are you kidding? I'm keeping everything in that tool kit like new. It hadn't been used when I bought the car, and I plan to keep it that way!

"I do all maintenance myself," said Mister X. "Wouldn't let anyone else near it. I don't even like to show it. I showed it once at Pebble Beach and got second place, but I really don't like it. It's not for me: I'd rather drive it than wrap it in cellophane!"

"When did you find out that it was the last one off the line?" I asked.

"Well, I knew from the beginning that it was a late car: I noticed the dates on the Borrani wheels. And a few years ago, a Ferrari historian saw it at the Historic Races at Laguna Seca, and he told me it might be the last one. But I wasn't convinced until I saw the complete list of numbers in the Miska Lusso book. It gives my car the historical prominence I wanted."

"By the way," I asked, "have you found any more Ferraris that you can fit into? Any other Ferraris you want to own?"

Before he could answer my question, his wife appeared, balancing three cups of coffee on a tray.

"Did you hear that question, Love?" he said.

"No, I didn't hear anything!"

"Do I fit another Ferrari beside the Lusso?"

"Yes, you fit in the Boxer. Why?" she asked, looking innocently at him.

"Oh, nothing." he said, and smiled back.

I got the feeling he was toying with the idea of getting one, but hadn't prepared his wife yet.

Quite a pair — the Lusso and the Boxer!

The Lusso was a magnet wherever it appeared. In the picture top left, possibly at the Frankfurt Show, it has just been uncrated. To the left, captured in an unknown location, it sports a for-sale sign as an encouragement to prospective buyers. The picture above shows the good-looking racing-style buckets, but the most intriguing features of the interior were the large tachometer and speedometer gauges. The center location was obviously a concession to styling – it was hardly practical. But then, driving a Ferrari, you don't want to know how fast you are going anyway! The engine compartment picture shows a well-restored example. (Photographs courtesy Road & Track.)

275 GTS

To Catch Ferrari Fever

There are so many ways to catch Ferrari Fever. So many dangerous sources of infection. They all have different degrees of future effect. Some get a mild case: others get it bad. Jim Hull got a severe case of the worst kind as a result of his first exposure to a Ferrari. It took place in Europe during the summer of 1962, when Jim was nineteen.

He had been going to school in Salzburg. When the term was over, all the other Americans hurried home. All but Jim, who had to make sure his Volkswagen got on a boat in Bremerhaven for eventual transportation to New York. Jim was supposed to follow a few weeks later.

He got to Bremerhaven late in the evening and spent the night in a youth hostel. There he happened to make friends with three other American students who had just come up with a bright idea — they were going to the twenty-four-hour race at Le Mans, and they were going to see it from the inside! They had no idea how this would be accomplished, but one of them lived in Santa Monica, Phil Hill's home town, and he personally knew the Champion of the World. (Or so he said.) Knowing the right people was all it took. That's what they thought!

This was just the thing for Jim. Forget that the car was due on the boat! He saw it as lucky coincidence that

Above, the prototype 275 GTS as photographed on Pininfarina's "turntable" in 1964. For the first-version production run, the front blinkers were changed to a wrap-around type and a side vent was added, of the same style as that used on the 330 GT 2+2. The second production version, pictured on the left, had a different side-vent design and a chrome strip below the door. (Photographs by Pininfarina, courtesy the Hilary Raab Collection.) The 1966 330 GTS, top right, received a longer nose like that of the 330 Coupe. (Photograph by Gordon Chittenden, courtesy Road & Track.) To the lower right, a Pininfarina photograph shows a curious-looking hardtop.

these guys needed transportation, and that he could provide it. The Volkswagen was turned south, now carrying four people.

They arrived in Le Mans several days before the start of the event. None of them spoke French, and the gendarmes spoke no English. But, by using Phil Hill's name frequently, they managed to get through to the paddock area, where they parked the car and put up their small tent.

They now turned their attention to the fascinating surroundings. Jim recorded it on film: the Jaguars, the Ferraris, the Maseratis, the engines, the mechanics, the Rodrigues Brothers — a circus of colors and beautiful forms. They were really on the inside! They had made it! But not quite yet.

On the morning of the race, Jim was brutally awakened at the ungodly hour of three o'clock. Two gendarmes had grabbed his legs, which, for lack of space, were protruding from the tent. The gendarmes shook him violently. Their car had been discovered lacking the obligatory sticker, and they themselves had no passes. They tried to explain, again using Phil Hill, but nothing seemed to convince the gendarmes. Suddenly, without conferring, the four ran off, disappearing in different directions. It was a long time before they dared to come out of their hiding places. They were eventually reunited, but now there was sin in Paradise!

They had to come up with a way to obtain those all-important passes. Maybe they could run errands for one of the drivers? Phil Hill's name came up again. But, being a member of the Ferrari factory team, he wasn't approachable. They turned to another famous American, Briggs Cunningham. He proved to be very polite, but he already had all the help he could use. As a last thought he suggested that they try Hugus and Reed.

Hugus and Reed? Who had ever heard of them? But they proved to be just the right ticket. They had a very informal setup: no mechanics, no timekeepers, no errand boys. They could certainly use the help of a gang of teenagers. The passes were finally secured; they had made it!

Hugus/Reed were to drive the same experimental Ferrari that Tavano/Baghetti had driven the previous year. The car had since been sold to Chinetti, who had campaigned it in the States. Stirling Moss had driven it to a fourth at Daytona. The car was later sold to enthusiasts in Chicago, who had now entered it at Le Mans. Jim never learned what kind of previous experience the drivers had, but he found them to be very happy and easy-going fellows. The car was beautiful

(continued on overleaf)

Shown first at the Paris Salon in October 1964, the 275 GTS, together with its companion, the 275 GTB, represented a new generation of Ferraris. The cylinder volume was enlarged, but more importantly, the cars now had independent rear suspension. They also came with a five-speed transmission and rear-mounted gear box. The featured 1965 model belongs to Jim Hull of Brentwood, California, and carries chassis number 07479. The 275 Spyder may not be Pininfarina's most flamboyant styling exercise, intended as it was for discreet grand touring only. But set against the violent formations of red California rock, and painted the vibrant Ferrari yellow, its elegant lines are brought out to their full eye-catching advantage.

and fast, but it was the sound of it that got to Jim. At the time, of course, he could not have known that historians would later consider this car the prototype for the legendary GTO.

The race itself turned out to be somewhat of a monotonous affair for the crew. Their car ran like a clock; they were in ninth place after fourteen hours. The Ferrari kept roaring by, lap after lap, hour after hour, right on schedule.

Jim and his friends were kept busy. Two of them had the job of showing standings to the drivers. Another handled the communications between these two and the pit crew. Jim was chosen to run between the scorekeepers and the timekeepers, making sure the latest information was at hand at all times.

Their Ferrari was in seventh place after eighteen hours of driving. Everything was going smoothly until two hours remained and it was time for the last change of drivers. When they were ready to take off again, the engine didn't want to start. Panic in the pit! The hood was thrown open and many frantic fingers tried to find out what was wrong. Finally a Maserati mechanic was rounded up. Soon the Ferrari sped off again — delayed one hour!

When the final scores were in it became clear that the Americans at Le Mans had fared very well. Phil Hill piloted the winning Ferrari, Cunningham drove the fourth-place Jaguar, Grossman the sixth-position Ferrari, and Hugus/Reed took ninth!

And Jim Hull had played a part in it.

As the years passed, the Ferrari memories were pushed deeper and deeper into Jim's subconscious. They were suppressed by the responsibilities of serious studies, but also by the sense of anti-materialsm that he developed along with so many young people of his generation. The Ferrari Fever recurred temporarily at the end of 1965, when Jim bought the October issue of *Car and Driver*. It had a picture of a yellow 275 Spyder on the cover.

I busied myself behind the wheel of Jim Hull's yellow 275 Spyder, keeping the engine at about 1200 rpm while giving it the proper warm-up. I listened to the sounds coming from under the hood in front of me, as well as the sounds from the two sets of twin exhaust pipes behind me. Jim sat down in the passenger seat, pointed at the oil temperature gauge, and indicated that it was all right to take off. I backed out, accelerated in first gear, and rolled the short distance to Sunset Boulevard — all while I eagerly took in the view. It was luxurious. The seats

The photographs on this page feature the 1961 GTO prototype, chassis number 2643. The car was driven twice at Le Mans, where Jim Hull's pit-crew experience gave him his first taste of Ferraris. From bottom to top, the car is shown in different disguises: painted red with Italian colors on the hood as raced at Le Mans in 1961; then at an unknown later date in a Pininfarina photograph; and, finally, painted white with a blue stripe as raced at Le Mans in 1962. (Photographs by Pininfarina, courtesy the Hilary Raab Collection.) Pictured on the right-hand page, the 500 Superfast. Very few examples were made between 1964 and 1966, at a $38,000 price tag.

were wide and upholstered in soft black leather. There was a strip of wood veneer across the length of the dash. The speedometer was on the left, the tachometer on the right. Between them were small gauges showing the oil pressure and oil temperature. Four more gauges were lined up in the center.

The stubby gear-shift lever had a contoured knob and was placed on the left side of the tunnel. It felt very precise, in spite of the rear-mounted gearbox. I liked the visual effect of the gate plate, an item inherited from the race cars. We were flowing slowly along with the traffic on Sunset. I had no trouble keeping it in third at the low speed; the engine was wonderfully flexible.

"I had never seen a 275 GTS until I discovered this one parked on La Cienega, " Jim said. "It was for sale. I had always wanted one, and my furniture factory had just begun to return some of my investment."

I crossed the bridge over the San Diego Freeway, turned right on the other side, and circled down the ramp onto the northbound lanes.

"I bought the Ferrari in 1972, and used it every day for the first five years," he continued. "Never had any major trouble. Only had it tuned up once! But finally it started to smoke. It still ran good, but I was embarrassed at the Ferrari speed meets. It looked bad! So I had the engine rebuilt recently."

It was getting too noisy to keep up the conversation, so we sank a little deeper into the seats and enjoyed the sound, the wind, and the attention in silence. I turned off on Highway 14 after about twenty minutes. The traffic thinned out and I dared to run it up to ninety. The Ferrari felt marvelously solid and stable on the road. I could have continued forever, but our destination appeared on the left.

I had chosen Vasquez Rocks, a well-known location among movie makers. I had scouted it earlier; now I only needed to position the car in relation to the sun. The violent forms of the red rock were a stunning contrast to the refined lines of Pininfarina's yellow sculpture.

It was this understated elegance that had me fooled before I drove the 275 GTS. Now I knew that the subtlety was only skin-deep. Jim must have read my thoughts. He took out a magazine from under the seat; the pages were turned to an article about the GTS. He read a sentence aloud.

"For all its concessions to creature comfort, this is a hairy, demanding GT car that will stretch to the skill of the most talented driver."

I reached for the magazine and turned to the cover. It was a *Car and Driver* from 1965.

The photo was of a yellow 275 GTS.

330 GTC

Music for Mechanics

"I'm probably the only guy in the world who's gone directly from a fifty-seven Chevy to a Ferrari Lusso! Do you know anyone else? It's a big step. It happened in 1966. I was twenty-four, and had owned the Chevy since my high-school days, so it was almost ten years old. I was definitely ready for a change of image. I had seen a metallic-blue Lusso in Estes Zipper's Ferrari showroom on Wilshire Boulevard in Beverly Hills. Every morning when I drove to work in my Chevy, and every time I had an errand during the day, and every evening when I drove home, I went out of my way to catch a glimpse of that gorgeous Lusso. The more I looked at it, the more my want turned to need!"

Larry Bloomer unlatched the hood of his red 330 GTC, and, while raising it, he continued to tell the story of how he acquired his first Ferrari.

"I was a salesman for Xerox at the time, and it had been a very successful year for me, but not quite successful enough to win first prize in our company's national sales contest. The prize was a new Mustang convertible. I knew all along that I had a good chance of getting it, but one guy was better. It must have been fate! The same day I got the bad news about the Mustang, the Lusso was taken out of the showroom window. That gave me such a shock that I made a U-turn in rush-hour traffic and parked illegally to see what had became of "my" Lusso. I was told that a potential buyer was to test the car the following morning, and the car was being readied. That night I couldn't sleep. I woke up early the next day and found myself pacing outside the showroom waiting for Zipper's arrival."

Larry was still holding on to the open hood. His eyes shifted back and forth between me and the many familiar parts of the engine as he spoke.

"They wouldn't let me drive it. They probably thought I was just another car-crazy kid. Otto Zipper himself finally took me on a short ride after I had convinced him I was a serious buyer. I can still remember the look on his face when I told him I wanted to buy it. He was probably even more surprised when I paid with cash."

His eyes traveled to the back of the garage.

"As you can see, I still own the Lusso. I drove it every

The 330 GTC, top left and right, had pleasing lines from all angles, but especially the profile and the rear quarter treatments, which were excellent. Pininfarina's styling made the car look both sporty and elegant. Elegance also characterized the interior, to the left, with its wide leather seats and veneer-covered dash. The 365 GTC, above, first shown in 1968 and produced until 1970, had only minor styling changes; the side vent was gone, but vents had been added on top of the hood. The engine compartment of the 330 GTC was dominated by the air cleaner, obscuring the view of the three Weber carburetors. (Photographs by de la Rive Box and Pininfarina, courtesy the Hilary Raab Collection.)

day for ten years — put more than 200,000 miles on it. Went through the engine twice. Completely refurbished it three times. Now it needs another cosmetic overhaul — I just haven't had the time, because I have been working on this one!"

His 330 GTC was pulled half-way into the garage. A beat-up Lusso rested behind it. Beside the Lusso, under a cover, I recognized the form of a Daytona. And back in a corner sat a 1957 Chevrolet.

"I still have the Chevy as well!" Larry said. "Just can't give up my old cars, I guess. Now when I get the garage finished, I'm going to restore the Chevy. I'm going to put all the cars back in their original shape. The Lusso needs a new paint job again, but the interior and the drive-train have already been redone. I'm almost finished with this 330."

Larry's new garage could hold eight cars. He had included an unusual feature for a private garage — a pneumatic hoist, just like the ones found in gas stations. I gathered he was planning to do some serious work here.

His home is located in Cheviot Hills, one of those hidden communities right in the middle of Los Angeles — an oasis in a vast desert of buildings and streets and cars. Here he is only ten minutes away from his office in Beverly Hills, where he is a commercial real estate agent.

"What was wrong with the 330?" I asked.

"It was smoking! What else?"

"Naturally! And you had to change the rings!"

"No! That's a mistake many Ferrari owners make. When the car smokes, they immediately think it's the rings, when that's actually not the problem most of the time. Most Ferraris are driven very little; therefore, the rings don't get that worn. The valve guides and/or seals, on the other hand, have always been a weak point. They get worn and allow oil to seep into the combustion chambers. That's what usually causes that embarrassing smoke!

"But how can you know without opening the engine whether it's the rings or the seals?" I asked.

"There are several ways. If the seals and/or the guides are shot, and the engine sits or idles for awhile, oil in the valve covers will run down along the valve stems and into the combustion chambers. When you fire up the engine, you get that big cloud of smoke."

"Yes, I understand."

"Replacing the valve guide seals is relatively simple and far less expensive than the major overhaul required to replace the piston rings. If you wanted to find out if the

(continued on overleaf)

Under the hood – 300 horsepower and handling to match; the 330 GTC could have done well on the race track had it not been for its weight. Well, it was not a coincidence. The 330 GTC was all Ferrari had intended it to be – a fast, reliable, luxurious, elegant-looking touring machine for two. As such, it was extremely successful – probably the most sensible Ferrari for everyday use to date. Owner Larry Bloomer knows what he is talking about – he has been driving Ferraris on a daily basis since 1969. His featured 1968 model, chassis number 10508, has just been totally overhauled by Bloomer. In the pictures, he takes it for the first test drive, choosing the Santa Monica Mountains with their steep grades and sharp curves; the location is just right for the occasion, all beautifully laid out as it is against the backdrop of the blue Pacific Ocean.

rings are bad too, you can run a compression test. You should get a compression reading on all twelve cylinders. The readings should be within plus or minus ten percent of each other. The hours on the engine will determine the actual pounds in the cylinders. If you get a reading outside the ten percent range, you still can't be sure it's the rings. It could be a leaking valve, for instance. Then what you do is squirt some oil into each cylinder so it surrounds the piston and covers the rings. Then take another compression reading. If it improves, you can be sure the rings are bad. The oil, you see, seals the space around the cylinders, preventing air from leaking past the piston. So if your compression is good, but it smokes bad when you fire it up, you can be pretty sure it's the valve guides and/or the seals. That's what was wrong with my 330 GTC. It had factory-installed seals that were worn out."

"And you replaced them yourself?" I asked. Dressed in his pin-striped suit, he somehow didn't look like he was capable of it.

"Sure. It's not that difficult. I did a lot of engine rebuilding during my high-school years. When I bought the Lusso I began spending a lot of time down at Zipper's. I used to watch the mechanics work and I asked them many questions. And I took notes of what I saw and heard. Richard Van DeWater was Otto's chief racing mechanic then. He was always willing to walk me through problems as he solved them. The complexity of the Ferrari engine is really a myth, in my opinion. It's not all that different from working on two six-cylinder Chevrolet engines with a common crank, if you know what I mean."

"I trust you. But I would never try it myself!" I said.

"It's reasonably simple, but quite exacting! First you make sure the car is in neutral. If it's left in gear, and you happen to bump into the car while working on it, you'll move the cylinders and mess up the timing. And that's bad news! Four degrees off and you bend valves. You start by removing the cover plate over the small opening in the bell housing, between the distributors. Through this opening you can see the flywheel. From the many marks on the flywheel, you can determine the cam, ignition, and valve timing. There is a mark for every cylinder's firing position and lots more. When you understand the marks, numbers and letters on the flywheel, it's like being able to interpret another civilization's language. If you follow it perfectly you will never go wrong. But enough of that. You make sure the number-one cylinder is set top dead-center A. The mark is PM 1/6 on the flywheel. Next, remove the carburetors, including their manifolds. Take off the distributor caps, but

The 330 GT 2+2 was a beautifully-balanced design, styled and built by Pininfarina. It was first introduced in 1964, with a four-headlight arrangement. It was rather uncharacteristic for Ferrari, and did add excitement to the front, but the model was not well-received visually. The outside, larger lights were the low beams, and the smaller were the high beams. The conventional Ferrari look returned the following year, and this model was produced until 1966. The interior followed the theme of the period with a wooden dash. (Photographs by de la Rive Box and Pininfarina, courtesy the Hilary Raab Collection.)

before going on, stop and be sure the rotor is firing the number-one cylinder. If not, rotate the engine 360 degrees to PM 1/6 again. The rotor should now be firing number one. Mark the distributor's bases where they bolt onto the engine, and mark on the distributor's housings exactly where the rotors are pointing before any removal. Now you are ready to tackle the valve covers. Then off with the timing-chain covers. You have to remember to insert wires to hold the timing chain so it doesn't fall down into the cam/timing sprockets. First you remove the rocker arms, then the sprockets and the cams. There you are! Ready to attack the valve guide seals. Doesn't sound too difficult, does it?"

"Are you kidding? That's too much for me," I said. "My head is spinning just from listening to you. Let's start it up instead. I've always wanted to know what makes all those noises. Can you tell them apart?"

"Sure. If you exclude the sound of the exhaust, there are three main sources of sound: first there is the noise of the adjusting screws at the tips of the rocker arms hitting the top of the valves. This sounds a little like constant surf washing against pebbles on the beach. The second source of noise are the roller arms. This sounds like a 'scheeeeeee.' The third source is the timing chain; it's a whining noise. It actually varies, depending on the engine rpm and how tight the chain is. The sound becomes more high-pitched the tighter it is. On the other hand, you can sometimes hear the chain hit the timing case housing when it's too loose."

Larry went behind the wheel and started up the 330 GTC engine, then came back with a rubber hose and a long screwdriver.

"Either of these makes a great stethoscope," he said.

He put the rigid hose on different parts of the engine, with the other end to his ear. He smiled and motioned for me to listen also.

"The screwdriver works almost as well. Start in the upper section here on the valve cover. Then place the other end of the hose near your ear, like this. Here, try it! Do you hear? That's the adjusting screws hitting the valves. Then move the hose down to the center part of the valve cover. That's where the roller bearings on the rocker arms and the cam are. Now move it to the timing-chain cover. Hear the difference?".

"Yes. Beautiful," I replied. "It's like an orchestra. Here are the drums. There are the cellos. And over there are the horns!"

Larry went back behind the wheel, revved up the engine, and all the sounds came together in harmonious metallic tune. He leaned out and grinned.

"Some music, isn't it?"

275 GTB 4

Heritage of a Yellow Shark

I have always been attracted to garages. Ever since my early childhood in Norway during World War II, when I was first introduced to the forbidden mystique of my grandfather's garage, I have felt that they played a vital part in my passion for cars. In the cold darkness of this childhood garage was stored a Model A Ford and a big black Buick. Behind the heavy doors, only to be opened during the night, lingered just the right blend of smells from rubber and gasoline. The few times I had been inside, it had always been against the expressed will of my grandfather, who feared that if it became known what he was hiding there, the Occupation forces would immediately confiscate his beloved treasures. He had not driven them since the first day of the Occupation.

Years later I would see more garages than I had ever dreamed of. One of the best was a garage in a sixteenth-century stone house in England. The floor was full of oil spots, all neatly covered with sawdust. There were tools and engine parts on the work benches. On the walls hung number plates from all the famous rallies in Europe. They had not been collected at swap meets — they were "the real thing." The owner had been a participant, sometimes capturing top honors, in both

The 275 GTB was unquestionably one of the most exciting cars conceived by the Ferrari/ Pininfarina team. The 1964 prototype is featured in the three photographs to the left. Notice that one side had a vent window, while the other lacked it. The picture above shows Pininfarina Senior with his beautiful creation. It also shows the original nose treatment, while the small photograph top right shows the frontal aspect of the new long nose introduced in the middle of the production run. With the appearance in 1966 of the four-cam engine, right, the 275 reached its climax. (Photographs by Pininfarina, courtesy the Hilary Raab Collection.)

the Monte Carlo Rally and the Tour de France, as well as in the Alpine Rally and many others. This car itself, a 1938 BMW 328, had belonged to the owner ever since it was brand new. And it was still the proud centerpiece of the garage.

One of the most charming garages I have seen recently belongs to Bruce Meyer of Beverly Hills, California. His house is located on a palm-lined street only blocks away from where Howard Hughes garaged his Packard Caribbean.

Parked there among all sorts of memorabilia, such as a swordfish caught in Acapulco, a World War II civil defense helmet, a beat-up duck decoy, Bruce's old motorcycle boots, a Champion Spark Plug sign, an old American convention banner, and two antique chests from Rosa Roma's traveling vaudeville act, is a small but well-chosen collection of cars.

All the way in the back rests a brown Mercedes-Benz 300 S Coupe. In the middle row, awaiting its turn at the paint shop, sits a once-silver Mercedes-Benz 300 SL Gullwing; parallel to it is a two-tone green Packard Dual-Cowl Phaeton. Easily-accessible in the front row are the "drivers:" a dark-metallic-green 427 Cobra, and beside it, the car I had come to see and photograph — a fly-yellow Ferrari 275 GTB/4.

Its engine was turning lazily at 900 rpm.

The 275 GTB/4 is one of my personal favorites. It embodies the best of two worlds — the classic and the modern. Its new concepts do not remove it too far from the old Ferraris, and the 275 engine is closely-related to the basic 250 design. Only it is more powerful now, thanks to the enlarged bore and the four-cam setup. It produces a healthy 300 hp at 8000 rpm!

The suspension is finally independent all-around. The design copies the race-proven 250 LM. The weight distribution is also improved, thanks to the rear mounting of the gearbox, which has five speeds. The front-engined Ferrari sports car has reached its ultimate stage of chassis development!

The styling combines the best from the TDF and the GTO. It is a most harmonious and well-balanced translation of these two classic forms. The new style expresses a powerful agressiveness, even bolder than that of the cars that inspired it.

The GTB can be said to be the culmination of Pininfarina's classic themes as they were seen in both his racing cars and his production models. The beautiful plexiglas-covered headlights are there — first used in

(continued on overleaf)

Race car-inspired – in fact, looking much like a fattened GTO with an LM nose – the 275 GTB was another in a succession of formidable street Ferraris with close kinship to cars campaigned on the racing circuit. A specially-prepared version won its class at Le Mans in 1965. With the introduction in 1966 of the four-cam engine, the car, in this form designated 275 GTB4, turned an already-powerful machine into pure dynamite. The 1967 model pictured on these pages, belonging to Bruce Meyer of Beverly Hills, carries chassis number 10615. Lacking high-speed driving opportunities suitable for such a car, the owner often finds himself seeking out other excitement – such as the thrill of hearing the sounds of the vee-twelve reverberating between narrow tunnel walls.

the mid-fifties on the Testa Rossa and others, and later decorating many a TDF and the GTO. The berlinetta roofline is there — inspired by the TDF, the SWB and GTO. The vents behind the side window are there — reminiscent of those on the TDF. The air vents in the side panel are there — taken directly from the GTO. The rear spoiler is there — derived from sports racing cars of the early sixties, and forwarded to the GTB via the GTO and the Lusso. And the nose is there — inspiration supplied by both versions of the GTO as well as the LM. Quite a heritage!

The GTB was first introduced with a short nose. This style was probably more in keeping with the intended visual balance between front and rear end. It also facilitated a larger, more classic-looking grille. But the short nose was found to be incapable of holding down the front end of the car. It would "float" and "skate" at high speeds. The new, long nose took care of this problem. It also gave the new 275 GTB that much-appreciated, aggressive shark look.

Bruce backed the 275 GTB out of its space next to the Cobra. I jumped into the passenger seat, armed with camera and note pad. It was not quite like Dennis Jenkinson getting ready for riding in the Mille Miglia with Stirling Moss in his 300 SLR, but it was still exciting.

The cockpit was small and race-car-like. This feeling was amplified by the way the slanted side window came close to my head. The round shape of the hood and fenders in front of me were carried on inside by the curving ends of the dashboard as it followed the bottom contour of the sloping windshield. The dials and their arrangement were inspired by the classic Ferrari style, and the old Nardi steering wheel was still the crowning centerpiece, just as it had been on a long line of great road cars.

Bruce took it very easy to start with, keeping the load on the engine to a minimum as we slowly drove down Beverly Drive. There were a lot of noises coming from the suspension. It sounded like we had a load of logs. I knew they would go away as soon as everything had warmed up. The ride felt stiff and good. We turned left on Sunset, and Bruce let the machine work a little harder. As we turned left on Doheny Drive, I noticed that he was still keeping an eye on the oil temperature gauge.

"The first owner of this car was actually Bill Doheny. His family was one of the original landowners around here. I believe much of Beverly Hills is built on land that once belonged to them. It's very fitting that we give it a test right here on Doheny Drive, isn't it?"

Bruce gave it more throttle as we approached a long

left-hand curve. We swept through it at about 4500 in third gear. I felt the road-hugging qualities of the car as I was pressed against the side of the door. But I knew it would be impossible in surroundings like these to find out what the car was really good for. It was somehow very discouraging when yellow signs reading "Max speed 25 mph" kept flashing by every so often.

"This is Graystone, the old Doheny estate," Bruce told me. "The American Film Institute uses it now. Let's see if they'll let the car through!"

The guard peering out from the gatehouse didn't seem to recognize the yellow monster that suddenly appeared in his field of vision. He shook his head and we had to back out.

"What's the world coming to when an old member of the family isn't welcome anymore?" laughed Bruce.

We turned left on Summit Drive. The road was parallel to a white wall. The wall unexpectedly curved to the right, following the road as it turned. Bruce stepped on the accelerator on a sudden impulse. The curve kept turning sharper and sharper. There was no way of seeing how it would end, because the wall was always there, obscuring the view. Bruce kept going at 6200 in second gear. The roar was terrific as it bounced back from the white wall. The road just kept on turning, but Bruce didn't want to let up. I was pressed up against his shoulder, leaning heavily with the car. I had no way of steadying myself, since my hands were full of cameras and pens. The tires were screaming and the wall kept coming closer; I was sure we would crash into it any moment. As suddenly as he had begun, Bruce let up on the accelerator and stepped on the brake. We came to a halt with smoking tires, just a foot away from the wall.

"Jeees! That was close! Do you know what this wall is?" Bruce looked at me with a wild expression.

"I have no idea!"

"This is Pickfair! It belonged to Mary Pickford, the queen of the silent movies. The most famous landmark around here. Can you imagine ruining the wall of Pickfair? How embarrassing!"

He grinned mischievously, and I suspected he had done it all on purpose.

We went down Coldwater Canyon Drive, crossed Sunset, and returned safely to Bruce's house, where we parked the Ferrari and immediately switched to the Cobra. The day wasn't over yet! I had to compare the stunning kick of Maranello's fullblood with the lethal bite of Detroit's brute.

We went up the hill, surrounded by a deep thundering roar, and crossed Sunset again, but this time we decided to avoid the street with the white wall.

The Ferrari sports car production has always been dominated by the Berlinetta theme. Consequently, the total output of true roadsters over the years has been quite small. One historian sets the figure at approximately 900. The 275 GTS/4, or NART Spyder, is an extreme example. This stunning beauty came about as a result of pressure from Ferrari's East Coast distributor, Luigi Chinetti. Regrettably, only ten cars were made. In these photographs by Stanley Rosenthal, the NART Spyder is tested for Road & Track by Ron Wakefield. Future editor-in-chief Tony Hogg is the passenger in the picture to the left. (Photographs courtesy Road & Track.)

365 GTB 4 DAYTONA

A Paperboy With Exotic Taste

It seems like some men are destined to own Ferraris. Is it determination or is it luck? Who knows? But somehow they always manage to keep at least one Ferrari around.

Steve Gilman is such a man.

Although still young, he has had his eyes or hands on more Ferraris these last few years than most fortunate enthusiasts will have in their lifetime.

It began in Florida when Steve was twelve. He can't remember when he first heard about Ferraris, or what occasion first sparked his interest, but he does recall how he fulfilled his dream.

"I woke up at five every morning and folded six hundred papers before I saw the sun. I was a paper boy with the largest territory in the entire Fort Lauderdale area. I made $300 a week. A week! That's a lot of money for a twelve-year-old."

We were sitting in the living room of his house, delicately attached to the steep hillside, high above Bel Air, California. Through the panoramic window, as wide as a cinema screen, I could see the entire San Fernando Valley, or as much of it as the haze permitted. Beyond the valley rose the blue silhouettes of the San Gabriel Mountains. It was an impressive view. But more provocative to me was the sight of Steve's red Daytona, decoratively parked in the driveway, just below the window.

"I put away money every week. I had one goal. I was determined to buy a Ferrari as soon as I could legally own a car. I was fourteen when I got my driver's license.

On my sixteenth birthday, I spent $7,500 on a used 250. It was red."

A naughty-boy smile lit up his face.

"The euphoria lasted a week. The Ferrari was too much of a temptation. This happened on one of the first evenings. I was showing off, I guess, going pretty fast. Too fast! Soon there were flashing red lights in my mirror. Instead of stopping I stepped on the gas. The combination of the Ferrari acceleration and my knowledge of the back-streets didn't leave the cops a chance. Remember, I was a paper boy, and this was my territory!"

The smile was replaced with a look of thoughtful disappointment as he continued.

"There weren't many fancy red sports cars in that part of town. Not with the kind of sound my Ferrari had. So it didn't take long before the police found out where I lived. My father sold it the next day . . . and he lost money on it too!

We were doing sixty on the Ventura Freeway. Steve was driving the Daytona. We were on our way to his company headquarters in Tarzana. He was just going to check on his messages before we continued north. We were going back into the mountains, where I had already found a location for photographing the Daytona.

I asked how he had come up with the idea for Style Auto, his line of automotive fashion products.

"My wife and I were relaxing in our room at the Plaza San Marco in Bergamo. It was late at night. Bergamo is an old resort in Northern Italy. It's a charming place that I'd like to go back to anytime. It's between Brescia and Milano — a good two hours from Ferrari.

"I was spending the day at Fiorano, Ferrari's test track in Maranello, watching the drivers set up the cars for a race. I forget which one. All I remember is that it was freezing cold all day. Then, late at night, the idea came to me like a flash! Why not make Ferrari sweaters! I got out a pen and paper and made some sketches, showed them to my wife and she liked them. Next day we went to a knitwear factory in Milano.

"We made the sweater green, the prancing horse red, and the Ferrari logo black. They came out beautifully! Later that week, we went to the Ferrari factory and gave some sweaters to Regazzoni and other team members. We gave some to Forgheri too. I've heard he passed one on to the old man himself. Don't know if that's true, but I like to think that he wears one of my sweaters when he's cold!

"That was the beginning. It was, of course, a long way
(continued on overleaf)

The 365 GTB/4 was the last front-engined vee-twelve sports car from Ferrari (unless this classic configuration returns at some future date). The pictures on the left-hand page show, bottom, the sleek profile; middle, the original headlight arrangement retained on the European version; top, the covered headlight design for the U.S. market. This page, top, a near-final-version prototype is tested somewhere in Italy. Notice the wheel-travel indicators and the unfinished headlight arrangement. Above and right, Chris Amon drives the 365 GTB/4. (Photographs by Pininfarina and Pete Coltrin, courtesy the Hilary Raab Collection and Road & Track.)

Described as a man's car, the 365 GTB4 may just be the ultimate in that category – at least if judged by the strength it takes to turn the wheel at low speeds. But this is deceiving, for the Daytona, so christened by enthusiasts after Ferrari's many victories in that race, only shows its true heritage – that of a race car – at very high speeds. If a woman can master the Daytona under these conditions, then it is a woman's car as well. The Daytona is in fact, more than any other production Ferrari, a driver's car. This 1972 model, chassis number 15175, photographed here high in the Santa Monica Mountains, belongs to Style Auto founder Steve Gilman of Tarzana, California.

from those first sweaters to full-fledged marketing, but the sweaters were the starting point. We then went into other items, like tote bags, driving jackets, hats and so on. But the sweaters were the beginning. There at the hotel room in Bergamo!"

We took off on Reseda and continued up to Oxnard. I asked Steve what he was doing in Bergamo besides coming up with bright ideas.

"This was on the tail end of the good old days when you could still buy inexpensive Ferraris in Europe. We found so many cars, I can hardly begin to recall them all. The rich Italians were afraid of driving them, you know. They had a sensitive political climate with terrorism and so on. It was best not to stand out from the crowd.

"We found one of the first Ferraris made. I think it was number 0012 and may have been driven in the Mille Miglia. The car was for sale. This contradicts what I just said about the situation in Italy, because the car was in Argentina. But the deal had to be made in Bergamo. The money was to be wired through Bolivia somehow — I can't remember all the details.

"We also bought a Bertone showcar made for Agnelli, the Fiat chief. And we bought a Testa Rossa. The most beautiful of them all, at least I thought, was the Neri and Bonacini Coupe. It's featured in the Fitzgerald/Merrit/Thompson Ferrari book. All of these cars were brought to the States where we found buyers for them. It was nice because we always had a lot of Ferraris around!"

We parked the Daytona and walked through the showroom. Gray walls and mirrors made an elegant setting for the Style Auto wares. Steve wasn't quite finished with his story. He sank down behind the desk in his office and continued.

"I think the most fascinating place I saw was an old stable at an ancient castle. It seemed like every stall was occupied by an old Ferrari. Imagine the frame of a 1950 car, just sitting there on the floor, covered with hay and dust. And get this! There was an old speed boat with a Ferrari engine!"

He was suddenly quiet, bending over a stack of red message notes. His mind was definitely on a different track now. He didn't even look up.

"I have too much to do here. Why don't you take the Daytona on your own and keep it all afternoon?"

I was surprised at myself. I had to control my reaction. After a pause I answered casually.

"Sure, Steve. That'll be fine."

The canvas-ripping came very easily, just by touching the accelerator. But the clutch was very hard and the steering was extremely heavy. I was trying to move out

The 365 GTB/4 was a ferocious competitor in long distance events. The photographs on these pages capture the Daytona in racing disguise on its major arenas – Le Mans and Daytona. Top left, Bell/Pillette took eighth place overall at Le Mans in 1972. Pictured left, Chinetti/Migault in car 38 and Posey/Minter in car 6, keep each other company during the 1973 Le Mans. Right, a NART-entered car during the 1974 Le Mans. Above, Paul Newman behind the wheel of Clint Eastwood's car in the 1977 Daytona race (Photos courtesy Road & Track).

of the parking space. Even if I didn't wear out the clutch, I knew my arms would be shot by the time I got the car moving. And where was the hood? It looked so long from the outside. Now I couldn't even see it.

But these negative characteristics disappeared as soon as I got on the freeway. I found that it doesn't matter if you can't see the hood when you know there is something that powerful under it.

I turned off on Topanga Canyon Road and onto Mulholland, going south. I was still driving in a proper, relaxed way, listening to the harmonious tune of the engine at 3500 rpm. To this day, I still don't know what come over me at the moment I discovered I had left the populated area.

I braked, shifted down to second and put my weight on the accelerator. The rocket took off! I let it wind up to 7000 rpm, then whipped the stick down to third. I can still recall the sound of the lever hitting metal at the end of the slot in the shifting gate. I was doing ninety in third.

Then I did the same thing over again. And again. I must be going crazy, I thought to myself. I had gotten nine tickets during the two years I owned an E-Type; they finally took my license away. And my insurance rates went sky-high. Now I had been clean for three years. Was I prepared to risk it all?

Things got somewhat calmer as the road began curving and climbing like in the Swiss Alps. Now I discovered a new game. I could utilize the enormous power of the car and the excellent weight distribution to whip it around the 360-degree corners. All I had to do was to give the car the right direction going into the curve, then control it with my foot going through it, letting the back end hang out.

For the photographs, I had chosen a spot at the top of the mountain, where the road curved around a cliff, overlooking a rocky moon-landscape. The mountain was rapidly turning violet in the setting sun; I had spent too much time driving. Now it was almost too late to take the pictures. I had to work very quickly. I looked in the view finder and saw the car where I had parked it in the middle of the curve. But there was something missing. I ran back to the car and turned on the headlights. They came up like the sleepy eyes of a giant monster from another world, and I immediately knew that was the look I wanted.

Afterward, when I drove my everyday transportation again, a Volkswagen Jeep, I had proof that the Daytona was from a different world — worlds apart from my Jeep. I found myself wondering what had happened to it. Why wasn't it moving?

SPYDER

First and Last of a Breed

Greg Garrison watched with satisfaction as his daughter Pat worked with the young stallion. There's no doubt, he thought to himself, that this horse has all the distinctive features of a pure Andalusian. Look at the eyes; see how intelligent and fearless he is. Look at the way he carries his head and the way he moves — like a nobleman from Spain.

The Andalusian still had the gray shading of a young animal; later, he may turn light silver dapple, or maybe he would become pure white, like his father. Legionario! Grand Champion of Spain! You have a good-looking son!

It was early morning. The sun had only moments ago appeared over the crest of the hills. Its warming rays would soon dry the dew in the fields of Hidden Valley, a horse-breeder's haven. In spite of its back-country atmosphere, it was less than an hour from the metropolis of Los Angeles.

Garrison, a veteran television producer and director, sipped his first cup of morning coffee while leaning against the white fence encircling the training rink. The air was still cool, but he could feel that the morning would turn into another warm day. The winter of 1972 has been mild so far, even for California, Garrison thought to himself, and the pleasant weather sure has continued into 1973, but we could use some rain soon.

Garrison walked over to the patio in front of the ranch house that was shaded by oak trees of the same size

and shape as those dotting the rest of the valley. The trees grew closer together down by the creek, where he kept the mares. The stallions were inside the stable. He sat down in a shaded chair, turned it so he could observe the entire rink, and took a sip of the coffee. He enjoyed the taste of the coffee and he enjoyed the freshness of the early-morning air and he enjoyed watching his daughter as she worked with the horse.

I have been very lucky, he thought to himself, but I have worked hard to make it happen. During those early years at Northwestern University, right after the war, I was already busy shaping my career. I wrote jokes for comedians then. Afterward I became involved with the drama school and after that came the years as an assistant stage manager on Broadway. One thing led to another. Broadway led to Hollywood. Hollywood led to the long and fruitful friendship with Dean Martin, which led to the production of the Dean Martin Shows, the specials with Frank Sinatra and many other television projects. Yes, I have been lucky! I have enjoyed it all and what's more, it has given me the means to pursue my other interests — purebred horses and purebred sports cars.

He looked across the rink, focusing on a sign of a prancing white horse attached to the wall of the stable. If you are a connoisseur of horses, you know that's the symbol of the Andalusians, he thought to himself, but you have to be a connoisseur of sports cars as well to know that the same prancing horse, in black, also decorates the Ferrari.

Garrison has owned a long string of sports cars. Among the British cars, he favored Aston-Martin; he has owned the DB 4, the DB 5, and the DB 6 models. Of the German cars, he was partial to Mercedes-Benz and BMW. He has owned a Gullwing, a 503, two 507s and many others. Of course, he has not escaped the attraction of the most distinctive and exotic of them all — Italy's Ferrari. He didn't own any Ferraris until the early sixties, when he had a Pininfarina Coupe, a Cabriolet, a 250 GTE 2 + 2 and a Superamerica. He purchased all of them as used cars. The new Ferraris came later. Now, in 1973, he had quite a collection of them.

He had known the people at the Ferrari factory since the mid-fifties — since the year he toured Europe with Esther Williams and the Aqua Spectacles. He produced shows in London, Paris, Rome and Milan. It was during this stay that he accepted an invitation to visit the Ferrari factory. He met Enzo Ferrari and Amerigo Manicardi, who was very important to his future dealings with the

(continued on overleaf)

First shown in 1969, the 365 GTS/4, or Daytona Spyder, was the last true Ferrari convertible. The yellow prototype is captured top left and right on its stand at the Frankfurt Show. In the 1972 photograph to the left, the Spyder shows off its top-up rear quarter view. Although extremely exciting to look at, the Spyder's true character is only fully revealed at speed; the combination of performance, handling, styling, and open-air charm makes it the ultimate drive for the road. To the right, the interior of a Daytona, with its compact cluster of gauges and uniquely-styled seats. (Photographs by Pininfarina and Geoffrey Goddard, courtesy the Hilary Raab Collection and Road & Track.)

End of an era! This is Ferrari's last true roadster, Ferrari's last front-engined sports car, Ferrari's last Daytona Spyder. Period. Pictured on these pages, chassis number 17073, delivered in 1974, is actually the last off the line. It belongs to Greg Garrison of Westwood, California, and has been driven less than 400 miles. It is a brand new car – and the owner plans to keep it that way. The styling of the Daytona was both classic and modernistic – a mix of stunning effect. Breathtakingly beautiful from any angle, the flowing simplicity of the enormous hood, the impossible rake of the windshield, the surprise angle of the cut-off rear – it all worked together as a coordinated whole.

Factory. Manicardi was Ferrari's man in charge of sales. They kept in touch over the years, and saw each other as often as possible. Garrison speaks of Manicardi, who has mastered seven languages, as his personal friend and one of the few Europeans he has met who understands and appreciates the American sense of humor.

In 1957, it was time for another visit to the factory. At that time, while he and Manicardi were talking in the courtyard, Pinin Farina happened to walk by, and Manicardi introduced him. Garrison commented on the Nashes that Farina had designed for the American market. Farina turned to Manicardi and told him in Italian that this American seemed to be quite a car enthusiast and that he really should own a Ferrari. Garrison was brought around a corner and there sat the prototype of the new Spyder. It had not yet been shown publicly. Garrison thought it was a most beautiful car, and soon afterward he regretted not having bought it. Many years later, he found the same car in Los Angeles; it is now a part of his Ferrari stable.

Garrison often met Enzo Ferrari during his frequent visits to the Factory, but it was always in passing. He was impressed by the proud posture, the firm handshake and the unyielding eyes. The word aloof is often used by others to describe Ferrari, but on one occasion, when Garrison was accompanied to the Factory by his young son Mike, he saw a different side of the man. Garrison noticed that Ferrari kept his eyes on Mike during the whole conversation. Almost ten years earlier, Ferrari had lost his only son to an incurable disease. The father's grief and the effect it still had on his daily life was well-known to the people around him, but it wasn't until later in the evening that Garrison understood the connection between Ferrari's interest in Mike and the memory of his own son Dino. After dinner, when they had already retired to their room at the Hotel Real-Fini, a large package was delivered, addressed to Mike. It was unwrapped and found to contain a collection of scale-model Ferrari race cars. A personal note expressed the sincere compliments of Enzo Ferrari.

Garrison purchased his first new Ferrari in 1966. He went to the Geneva Salon that year and was so taken by the new 330 GTC on the stand that he told Manicardi that he wanted that car! He didn't get the prototype, however, but he did get the first one off the production line.

Again, in 1968, as soon as Garrison heard of a new model being shown in Paris, he called Manicardi and told him that he was interested in the new four-cam car. A few days later, Manicardi called back and reported that he had spoken to Mister Ferrari about the matter,

Pictured above, the Daytona engine compartment, and to the left, Daytona engines at the Factory To the right, bottom, a one-off experiment from Pininfarina. The Targa top over-complicated the clear look of the Daytona. The remaining pictures on the right-hand page feature the 365 California, a Superfast-inspired four-seat convertible shown at the 1966 Geneva Salon and available on a limited-production basis during 1967. It had the single-overhead-cam engine and a rigid rear axle. The clear styling was marred by pop-up high beams, over-developed taillight treatment, and an out-of-place two-tone interior. (Photographs by Pininfarina and Pete Coltrin, courtesy the Hilary Raab Collection and Road & Track.)

and that Mister Ferrari wanted Greg to have a very special car — the prototype Daytona. This car was also on display in Geneva and London as well as in Los Angeles. Afterward, it was flown back to Italy, where Scaglietti replaced the interior and Ferrari mounted an engine, since the show car had only a mock-up engine under the hood.

Later, Garrison would own four Daytona Coupes in succession. Because of an old football injury to his arm, the Daytona, with its heavy steering, was a difficult car to drive in the Los Angeles traffic. But every time he sold one of those Daytona Coupes, he immediately regretted it and ordered a new replacement.

There was coffee left at the bottom of the mug, but it was cold now, and he had just decided to go inside for a refill when the telephone rang. He heard it through the open window and answered it on the fifth ring, wondering who would call so early.

"Good morning!"

Garrison immediately recognized the voice. Manicardi was calling from Italy. It was late there.

"Good afternoon, my friend! What's up?"

"I have an offer you can't refuse. We have five Daytona chassis left. I have talked to Ingegniere Ferrari, and we have decided what to do with them. Four cars will go to our Swiss distributor and we thought you might want the fifth!"

"I don't think so, Amerigo! I already have a Daytona!"

"These are all going to be Spyders, Greg! The Swiss distributor said he wouldn't sell theirs for five years."

There was a pause, then Garrison replied.

"Okay, Amerigo! Let me have the last one! I won't sell it, and I won't drive it for ten years! How's that?"

"I'm happy!"

"Okay! Have it painted in the special Pininfarina color, Oro Chiaro. And let me know when it's ready. I want to pick it up myself."

The Spyder will fit perfectly into my collection, Garrison smiled as he replaced the receiver. I already have the first production convertible; now I will also have the last. He walked over to the stable. I better ride Legionario now before it gets too hot. Then I'll take the Daytona into Hollywood.

His daughter was just returning Legionario's son to the stable.

"He really is a distinctive Andalusian, Pat!"

"He is beautiful, Dad!"

Yes, Greg Garrison thought to himself, he has those distinctive features that make him stand out. Just like the prancing horse on the grille of a Ferrari.

365 GTC 4

A Ferrari Brotherhood

We drive rapidly down Victoria Avenue, the grand old tree-lined esplanade cutting straight through Riverside's valley floor. Orange trees laden with ripening fruit surround us. Long ago, the area between the two lanes was set aside as an equestrian trail. I can visualize the wealthy landowners in their turn-of-the-century outfits, complete with wide-brimmed Panama hats and long cigars, parading on their purebred horses early in the mornings. Somewhere along the way, needless to say in the name of progress, the riding path was replaced by a double row of power poles. And today, in a further erosion of nostalgia, the orange groves are being cut down to make room for mushrooming housing developments.

But Victoria Avenue still has charm and beauty. Majestic crowned palms and gigantic eucalyptus, with branches meeting across the lanes, form long and cool tunnels. The silver-blue Ferrari 365 GTC/4 runs effortlessly through the shadows like a sleek, modern-day horse.

I'm accompanying the Rouhe brothers to Lake Mathews. We plan to do some serious driving on the network of roads surrounding it. It's a hot afternoon. The speed-wind flows soothingly through the open windows. We could have used the air conditioning, but that would have closed out the sound from the four exhaust pipes, and we definitely want to hear that purebred vee-twelve noise. The engine revs at just the right speed, and for some reason I find the exhaust note particularly satisfying around 4200 rpm, in third gear.

"This is a long way from Africa!" Ed says suddenly.

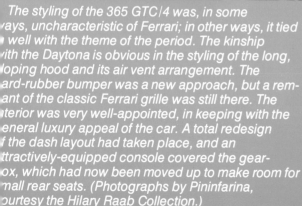

The styling of the 365 GTC/4 was, in some ways, uncharacteristic of Ferrari; in other ways, it tied in well with the theme of the period. The kinship with the Daytona is obvious in the styling of the long, sloping hood and its air vent arrangement. The hard-rubber bumper was a new approach, but a remnant of the classic Ferrari grille was still there. The interior was very well-appointed, in keeping with the general luxury appeal of the car. A total redesign of the dash layout had taken place, and an attractively-equipped console covered the gearbox, which had now been moved up to make room for small rear seats. (Photographs by Pininfarina, courtesy the Hilary Raab Collection.)

He is behind the wheel. Richard sits in the passenger seat. I occupy the two small back seats. My six-foot-one body is squeezed in diagonally, equally distributed between the two seats. I had insisted on trying them for myself. In a fold-down position they make an adequate space for luggage, but as seats they are definitely only for children.

"Yes, this is certainly far from Africa!" Richard repeats. "Thirty-five years and eight thousand miles away. Who would have guessed when we were kids and drove that home-built go-cart in the middle of the African jungle that we would end up in Riverside collecting Ferraris?"

"That go-cart was the most primitive vehicle since the invention of the automobile," Ed recalls. "We wrote to friends in the States and asked them to ship us a lawn-mower engine. They sent us a Briggs & Stratton. I think it came off a surplus Army generator. Everything else on that go-cart was made out of wood. It had a wooden frame, wooden wheels and a wooden steering wheel. Everything was wooden!"

"Remember that dusty road we drove it on?" Ed asks Richard.

"Yes, we filled the carburetor with gas and went as far as we could on that dirt road. The natives were running alongside, frightened but intrigued. When we ran out of gas, they helped us push the go-cart back for refueling. Then we took off again!"

"Where was this?" I asked.

"In the Belgian Congo — it's called Zaire now — at the Songa Mission," Ed answers. "Our parents were missionaries there. The nearest town was four hundred miles away!"

"A very unusual place for developing an interest in cars!" I say. "What kind of vehicles did they drive there in the Belgian Congo? Land Rovers?"

"No, I never saw any Land Rovers. I recall only American cars," Richard answers. "I remember a gray forty-seven Pontiac that we had there at the Mission."

"I remember one time when the entire family went to Cape Town in South Africa," Ed continues. "We had to pick up two new cars there. One of them was a Plymouth and the other was a Chevrolet; they were forty-eights. We boys helped drive them back. It was a three-thousand-mile trip!"

"We were crazy about collecting brochures!" Richard remembers. "We had our friends in the States send them to us. And we cut out pictures from magazines that we got. They were usually half-a-year old by the time they reached the Congo, but we were still able to keep up with the new models."

(continued on overleaf)

Civilized is the word used to charac-
terize the 365 GTC4. And civilized it is –
from the soft leather seats and the
effective air conditioning to the
power-assisted brakes. But don't
be mislead by such amenities. Under
the hood hides a very powerful four-cam vee-
twelve. It takes two rows of three twin-throat carburetors to feed the 330 horses. The 365 GTC4 is
a worthy, often underestimated, touring companion to
the Daytona. This 1972 model, chassis number
15653, was photographed among ripening citrus
trees and tall palms in Riverside, California. The
silver-blue beauty belongs to the Rouhe brothers, Ed
and Richard, both experienced Ferrari enthusiasts
with a stable to choose from.

We're on the freeway now. Ed lets the Ferrari run free. "I only drive the Ferraris when I know I can go at least 100 mph," he says. "When I'm past eighty, I begin to feel what a Ferrari is all about. 'Aha!' I say to myself, 'this is what a Ferrari was made for!' "

We turn off the freeway now and continue on a two-lane road. I soon see the lake on my left. Ed is quiet while he negotiates a long left-hand curve.

"So, there you are in Africa, driving and getting excited about American family sedans!" I say. "What about sports cars in general, and Ferraris in particular? When did you first become involved with them?"

"Well, we didn't know about them until we got back to the States and started reading Road & Track," Richard responds. Ed is still busy with that long curve. A sharp right-hander comes up ahead.

"I drove my father's MGA to begin with," Richard continued. "Then, I bought an Austin-Healey and later, a Jaguar E-Type. The first Ferrari was a 275 GTB/4. Ed talked me into it; he got one also. They were both red. Then came five 365 GT 2 + 2s and a Daytona Spyder. All we have right now is this 365 GTC/4, a 308 GTB, and two Daytona Coupes."

"And you own them together?"

"Yes, we started out together as car enthusiasts in Africa; we might as well continue to share that interest. Besides, we're both Ferrari men. We like the same kind of car!"

The road divides in two. Ed goes left. He stops the car after a few hundred yards on the narrower road. I see it continue curving up a hill ahead of us.

"Now it's your turn to drive," he says to me. "I'll sit in the back for awhile!"

I crawl out from behind the passenger seat and stretch my legs while walking around the Ferrari. The styling of the 365 GTC/4 is a curious combination of soft lines and sharp edges. From the rear, for instance, it looks quite square. If you see it from the front and side, on the other hand, it looks rounder. The curving line that starts low at the nose and arches over the front wheel, sinks as it passes the cockpit, then makes another arch over the rear wheels before it sinks again, is mainly responsible for this appearance. The styling of the front bumper also adds to the impression.

"The car is really very beautiful!" I say to Ed as we meet behind it en route to our respective new seats.

"Yes, it is!" Ed says. "There's no question that it was overshadowed by the Daytona while they were both in production. Only now is the GTC/4 beginning to become widely-appreciated."

Ed squeezes into the rear seats. I make myself com-

The photographs on this page show the 365 GT 2 + 2, introduced at the Paris Salon in 1967. Produced between 1968 and 1970, it was the most advanced four-seat Ferrari so far, featuring independent rear suspension, ventilated disc brakes, power steering and power windows, as well as air conditioning. In spite of its weight, it could move four persons at a top speed of 152 mph! Pictured on the right-hand page, the latest of the 2 + 2 Ferraris, the 400 Automatic – a further development of the 365 GT/4 2 + 2 first seen at the Paris Salon in 1972. (Photographs by de la Rive Box and Pininfarina, courtesy the Hilary Raab Collection and Ferrari S.p.A.)

fortable behind the leather-covered steering wheel and adjust the seat until I'm sitting the proper distance from the wheel.

The dash, compared with the Daytona's, is totally different. It was designed very tastefully. It's covered with the same dark gray, cloth-like material used in the Daytona. After a few years in the California sun it tends to fade, but in this car it's still perfect.

A rather bulky but attractive console rests on top of the gearbox, which has been moved forward to make room for the back seats. It could more fittingly be called a comfort console; the switches and buttons all have to do with the air conditioning, the radio, the heat and cold air ventilation, the power windows and the front and rear window defrosters. There are even individual fans for each side of the cockpit.

The centerpiece of the console is the gear-shift lever. It's not gated, as it is on the Daytona, and the layout is also different; on the GTC/4, first gear is located forward, which is the position for reverse on the Daytona.

I give it throttle and let go of the clutch. It's the typical Ferrari clutch. You have to be assertive and let it up in one decisive movement, or else you'll be taking off in embarassment. The wheel feels a little too light for my taste, owing to the power assist. I shift to second. Then I make a mistake that has to do with the lack of gate, but mostly with my lack of experience with the car: I go directly from second to fifth! That's a true let-down. It's a painful anticlimax to the normally very-satisfying acceleration process. I slow down and do it over again, getting it right this time. All four of them! It feels very good.

The GTC/4 is smooth and responsive, not as brutally-powerful as the Daytona, but quite adequate. I move up into the curvy and hilly part of the road now. I shift down to second. A particularly inviting turn is coming up. I give the car full throttle in the middle of the corner, and *swish!* The back end spins out! No problem. I just let up a little on the gas and the car takes care of it; I'm back on the track as quickly as I got off it.

"Did that scare you?" I say, and glance over my shoulder with a smoothing-over smile. At that moment I see something red out of the corner of my eye.

"No — not at all! It's hard to do anything wrong with this car," Ed says while struggling to regain his balance in the back seats.

I look in the rear-view mirror. I can't believe my eyes. There's a bright-red Lamborghini Miura right on my tail. It wants to pass. I make room, and it shoots past me in a way that makes me look like a Sunday driver.

"That's our kid brother," Richards says. "He's a Lamborghini man!"

246 GTS DINO

The Dino Legacy

The age of eleven could very well be the magical time for a young man's introduction to the world of motoring. It was at this age that Enzo Ferrari for the first time went on his own to watch the 1909-vintage race cars duel on the highway outside Modena. Together with other similar occurrences, this experience led Ferrari to a career which, in the history of racing, will never be surpassed.

The eleventh-year experience of Bart McGrath, however, having had no effect yet on the course of history, would seem too insignificant to mention were it not for the fact that the retelling of such events serves as nostalgic reminders to all enthusiasts.

Bart grew up in Dartford, an industrial suburb south of London. The family lived a quiet life. They rarely deviated from their established routines, and couldn't afford to spend money on extravagant pleasures. Young Bart could have stayed locked into the same environment had it not been for Mister Bishop, the next-door neighbor.

Mister Bishop was an eccentric and an adventurer. He had been a pilot during the war. Now, when it was over, he found that nothing could match his death-defying experiences in the sky. In 1949, in an effort to recapture some of the excitement lacking in his life, he acquired a 1934 Bullnose Morris.

The car needed extensive work, and Mister Bishop spent all his spare time on the project, sometimes working late into the night. Young Bart assisted in any way he could, but he generally had to go to bed very early. Worried about how Mister Bishop was managing without his help and company, Bart usually never fell asleep until the voice of Mister Bishop's wife shattered the quiet night, demanding that her husband come to bed at once,

Pictured on this page, the 1966 365 P, a Paris show car and one of several experimentals carrying the pre-Dino look. The 330 P3, at the top of the right-hand page, was typical of the mid-engined sports racers of the era, which provided the basic inspiration for the Dino shape. To the right, a portrait of Ferrari's only son, Dino, as it still hangs on the wall in Ferrari's private Maranello office. To the far right, middle, the rear-window treatment, reminiscent of the Dinos, of a one-off show car. Bottom, far right, a coupe forerunner to the Fiat Dino Spyder, which was also powered by the Dino engine. (Photographs by Pininfarina, courtesy the Hilary Raab Collection. Dino portrait by Gunther Molter, courtesy Road & Track.)

or else!

One day, the Bullnose was ready to drive. Mister Bishop asked Bart if he would like to come along on the maiden voyage. He was planning a trip to the Daily Express Trophy Race at Silverstone. Bart had seldom been beyond Dartford, let alone seen an international race; he accepted at once, but his parents were very concerned. Are you going in that old car? For sure it will break down! In the end, however, seeing the enthusiasm of the boy, they let him go.

After a trouble-free drive, during which Bart was indoctrinated with talk about British racing heroes, they arrived just in time for the beginning of the race.

Bart was excited as never before. His eyes darted from one point of action to another, then came to rest on the sleek, open-wheeled race cars as they lined up for the start. His level of excitement rose even higher as soon as the race got under way. He was immediately disappointed, however, when a red car took the lead over the green ones and held the position with ease.

Every time this car came shooting toward the end of the straightaway and rounded the corner in a perfectly-controlled four-wheel slide, Bart focused on the driver, who was clearly visible in the low-cut cockpit. The thin fabric helmet and the aviator goggles made him look like the heroes Bart had seen only in photographs. He wore a sleeveless shirt, and Bart noticed the play of the muscles in his tanned arms and the firm grip of his gloved hands on the steering wheel as he forcibly kept the car on its course.

The nose of the car was flat and covered by an egg-crate grille. It had two rows of louvers on each side of the spool-shaped body. The long exhaust pipes came out from below the engine and ran along the bottom of the body, ending behind the rear wheels. The car was attractive in a no-nonsense way, but in Bart's opinion, the sound was the best part. He listened with fascination to its distinctive roar as the car accelerated up the straightaway in front of the bleachers. With every lap his initial resentment gradually turned into admiration.

Mister Bishop told him that this was a new Italian make called a Ferrari. The cars had already won several races on the Continent. It was Alberto Ascari, their top driver, who again drove it to victory! The car had a super-charged engine with twelve cylinders in vee-formation, Mister Bishop told Bart, who did not understand the terminology, but understood that the car had to be supreme in order to have beaten the British. So it was that, at the magical age of eleven, Bart first heard the two names he would forever keep in his memory —
(continued on overleaf)

Street legal? By the mid-sixties, the cars competing in international sports car racing had taken on shapes that looked less and less like the cars available for street use. Consequently, when the Dino was introduced in 1967, first in the form of the 206 GT, it came as a stunning surprise. Enthusiasts wondered if it was really intended for the road. The Dino, named after Ferrari's son, looked just like a race car; it had a mid-mounted racing-proven vee-six and superb handling to match that incredibly low, aerodynamically-effective styling. It was indeed a Ferrari for the road, and Bart McGrath of Huntington Beach, California, owner of the featured 1974 246 Spyder, chassis number 07470, didn't wait long to make up his mind. He wanted one – or two, rather! He now owns one Coupe and one Spyder – a great idea when you can't decide which one is the most attractive.

Ferrari and Ascari.

Alberto Ascari captured the World Championship in 1952 and again in 1953, both times in Ferraris. Two years later he was dead, the victim of a freak accident at Monza. He had borrowed Castelotti's Ferrari for a few practice laps. Driving without a helmet, he died instantly when the car, for reasons never established, overturned in a long left-hand curve. Ascari had driven for Ferrari as early as 1940, and although he was not on the team at the time of his fatal accident, his death was a terrible blow to Ferrari. But the tragedy would not come alone!

Ferrari had become a father relatively late in life. His only son, Dino, was his pride and joy. Dino had inherited the passion for cars and racing, and his father groomed him for an active part in the business. But Dino, who had long suffered from poor health, fell victim to an incurable kidney disease. He died on June 30, 1956, just over a year after the death of Ascari.

Dino, however, left a legacy. Before his death, even at his bedside, father and son had worked together with Vittorio Jano on plans for a new engine. Following Dino's suggestion, a vee-six configuration had been chosen. After Dino's death, Ferrari announced that the engine would carry Dino's name.

This engine was first planned for the new Formula Two class introduced in 1957, but the original 1489 cc displacement was soon enlarged to 2417 cc. In this form it became the power source of a new Formula One car, the 246 Dino. Mike Hawthorn captured the 1958 World Championship in this car.

After two unsuccessful seasons, the engine was placed amidships in a new car for 1961. It carried Phil Hill to a World Championship. After a disastrous 1962 season, which saw the demise of the vee-six Dino as a Formula One engine, it made a comeback in 1965, now used solely for sports-car racing, and it won the European Hill-Climb Championship Series twice. The 206 S was, with its mid-engine configuration and its distinctive styling, the direct inspiration for the soon-to-follow production version.

The new regulations for the 1967 Formula Two class required that the engine used be produced in no less than 500 examples. This was an impossible task for Ferrari; he turned to Fiat for help. The design was a Rocci-developed version of the original vee-six. The light-alloy components were produced by Fiat, but assembled by Ferrari. The new engine saw use in Ferrari's 206 SP sports racer, and appeared in two Fiat sports cars introduced in 1967.

Pininfarina had in 1965 already displayed a styling

All the sensuous beauty of Pininfarina's styling, translated into steel by Scaglietti, decorates these pages. To the right, bottom, the 206 GT, the first production version introduced at the 1967 Turin Show. This model was not available on the U.S. market. To the left, bottom, the 246 GT, introduced in 1969. Although it was built on a 40-mm longer wheelbase in addition to many other technical changes, its exterior was distinguishable from its predecessor only by minor details. The Spyder version, with removable roof panel, followed in 1972. (Photographs by Pininfarina, courtesy the Hilary Raab Collection and Ferrari S.p.A.)

exercise based on the Dino. Ferrari now assigned the final design work for the production car to the Turin firm. The 206 GT, first shown in 1966, had the engine mounted parallel to the length of the car. The light-alloy-bodied production version 206 GT was introduced in 1967. The engine had been turned to a transverse position.

The final version, the steel-bodied 246 GT, became available in 1969. Only minor styling details set it apart from the 206 GT, but mechanically there were important differences. It still had the same four-cam engine, but it had been enlarged. The block was now made from cast iron, and the transmission arrangement had been changed.

The 246 GT became the first "low-priced," "mass-produced" Ferrari. Its exotic styling and mechanical sophistication, combined with superb handling and excellent performance, made it a worthy monument to the memory of Ferrari's son.

I drove Bart McGrath's yellow 246 Dino Spyder southbound on the Pacific Coast Highway. The sun had long ago disappeared into the ocean. When it had become too dark to take any more pictures, Bart and I had gathered up the polishing rags and the film wrappers, and we were now on our way from the shooting location in the Santa Monica Mountains back to Huntington Beach, where Bart lives nowadays, far from his native England.

The 246 felt marvelously stable and massive. Its go-cart-quick steering wheel and spine-thrilling accelerator made it a pure pleasure to drive. Equally enjoyable was the view from the tightly-hugging driver's seat. I glanced at the illuminated gauges, neatly organized within an ellipse of brushed aluminum. In front of the wide, curving windshield, I noticed only a hint of the hood, but the ballooning fenders were adequate compensation They made me feel like I was driving the original Ferrari 206 racer!

We had removed the roof panel, and as I accelerated, I felt the cool, salt-smelling ocean air tugging at my hair. It was the perfect medicine after a day in the burning California sun. Bart, for once demoted to the passenger seat, turned to me with a big satisfied grin on his face.

"Any doubts about this being a Ferrari?"

"The heritage is there, the look and feel are there, but the name badge is missing!"

"That's the way it was planned. The small Dino is the offspring of the big Ferrari. A son is the offspring of his father, but he still has his own identity. Sentimental, but that's the way Enzo wanted it!"

BB 512 BOXER

A Boxer In The Wild

I stand in the middle of a narrow road, somewhere east of Kiowa, southeast of Denver. I hold my heavy camera with both hands. I look down at a point in front of my feet, focus on the yellow divider line, and follow it with my eyes as it stretches along the center of the arrow-straight road. I follow it until it becomes too faint to separate it from the gray asphalt surface, when I instead follow the road itself, until it also becomes too faint.

I'm waiting for the red Boxer to return. I have already photographed it from behind. Now I want to shoot the front view. The road was too narrow for the Boxer's turning radius, so John made a run down to a crossroad three miles ahead.

Besides the gray of the road and the yellow of the divider line, there's only the endless green of the surrounding prairie, the even-greater vastness of the blue sky, and the almost-transparent white of the clouds. They sail slowly in a northeasterly direction. The warm wind blows the same way, producing the only sound and movement in the quiet stillness as it shakes and shifts the tall grass. The road is the only man-made element in sight, until suddenly a red object appears on the horizon. I watch it grow.

The red Boxer belongs to John Dekker, thirty-six years old, nightclub owner, big-game hunter and race

driver. He drove cars when he was fourteen, built "street-rods" when he was sixteen, and raced "funny cars" professionally for eight years, four times becoming Division-Five Champion of the National Hot Rod Association.

During his active "hot-rod" racing career he piloted cars that accelerated from zero to 240 miles per hour in less than seven seconds. Lately, in an effort to recapture some of that thrill, he has again taken up racing, now driving a new Lola T 540 in Formula Ford.

When he wasn't racing, he was selling cars with the same success. One year, he became the leading new-car salesman in a region covering eleven states. Step by step, he invested his earnings in a business with a great potential; he also got himself a Ferrari 308 GTS, and took up big-game hunting in Africa and South America, always looking for excitement and new fields of challenge.

The red object becomes larger and larger. It looks like a scene in a movie, shot with a telephoto lens. The car bounces with the changing elevation of the road. I measure the light and check the setting; sixteen and a sixtieth. I can now vaguely hear the sound of the Boxer engine above the wind.

Last January, John decided to sell the 308. It wasn't that he didn't like it; in fact, he enjoyed this Ferrari so much that he wanted to take the step up to the ultimate Ferrari — the Boxer. He made his plans for the purchase, as always, with great care. He visited several of the shops which specialize in legalizing exotic cars. He compared prices and quality of workmanship. He wanted to be able to follow the work process and make sure that it all conformed to his standards.

Ferrari's super-car, the mid-engined Boxer, was first displayed at the 1971 Turin Show. The production version of the 365 GT/BB became available in 1973. The unique picture at the top of the left-hand page shows an early scale model. Compare this with the final shape of the prototype photographed on Pininfarina's "turntable." Above, the Boxer is undergoing aerodynamic testing. The 512 GT/BB was unveiled at the Paris Show in 1976. Among the exterior changes was the well-louvered rear deck, which improved the ventilation of the engine bay; compare the two bottom-row pictures, the 365 to the left, and the 512 to the right! (Photographs by Pininfarina and Pete Coltrin, courtesy the Hilary Raab Collection and Road & Track.)

The Boxer closes in quickly now. I hear John downshift to fourth, and now again to third. He's still going fast. I wave him over to the middle of the road. He understands and lines the car up along the center line. I see the Boxer move sideways with typical mid-engine quickness. The sound becomes strong and good now as John revs up and down-shifts to second. He's still going fast. Too fast? Maybe he has brake failure? Maybe he wants me to move? Now he brakes hard and comes to a stop twenty feet in front of me. I move up close; the fifty-five-millimeter wide-angle lens is on the camera. I look in the viewfinder, moving up and down and sideways, searching for the right angle and the right reflection. The all-red Boxer looks perfect. John ordered

(continued on overleaf)

Colorado's wide-open roads, cutting arrow-straight through the unpopulated prairie, were the perfect testing grounds for this brand new Boxer. Here the top speed of Ferrari's fastest, close to 190 miles per hour, could be reached without the risk of certain costly and irritating interruptions. John Dekker of Denver, owner of this 1980 BB 512 Boxer, chassis number 31157, took delivery at the Factory. He then made sure his treasure got safely on the plane to Los Angeles, where the necessary legal conversions were made. The graphic starkness of the surrounding prairie effectively contrasts Pininfarina's exquisite styling; masterfully-sculptured forms make the Boxer look just as resourceful as it is.

it that way from the factory. It looks much better than having the lower half of the body painted black. I take two rolls of ten shots each, bracketing up and down, then walk up to the car on the passenger side, open the door and sit down. I want to wait until later, when the sun is lower, to take the remaining shots.

"Were you testing me or the brakes?"

"Did you think I was going fast there at the end? I was just checking to see if you were paying attention."

"Good thing I was," I kidded. "How's the car running?"

"Perfect. But I'm taking it very easy. It's the first time it's been driven, you know."

"You picked it up in Italy, didn't you?"

"Yes, at the Factory. Well, in Modena, actually. Vern Lindholm was with me. He owns the shop where the legalizing was done, Ferrari Compliance in Santa Ana. We flew into Milan and took the train to Modena. The sales manager, Mister de Franchi, took us on a tour of the plant. During the tour we could hear the sounds from the test track nearby as the race cars were being set up for the Long Beach Grand Prix. We were introduced to Scheckter and Villenueve afterward in the restaurant across the street."

"Did you drive your car in Italy?"

"No, unfortunately not. We had planned to drive it to Rome, but something was wrong with the insurance papers. The Ferrari people just started it up there in the courtyard so I could hear it run. They then took it on a transporter to the Rome airport."

"You had it flown back?"

"Yes, I was on the same plane. I supervised the loading as well. We flew it directly to Los Angeles, so Vern could start on it right away."

"What all had to be done to make it legal?"

"Well, there are two sets of regulations you have to comply with. Structurally, first, you have to strengthen the doors and the bumpers to make them more crash-resistant. Fifty-pound steel bars are normally put inside the doors, but Vern has designed units that use corrugated eighteen-gauge sheet metal that weigh only five pounds and are just as strong. He's also designed special sheet metal assemblies that fit perfectly inside the original resin bumpers. With Vern's approach, you can hardly see any difference from the outside."

"What about the engine?"

"Well, that's the other set of regulations you have to comply with. You have to install a catalytic converter. Vern has a special unit manufactured to his specifications. You also have to install an air pump, designed to force air into the exhaust manifolds to improve the burning of excess fuel. A pair of doors also has to be installed

inside the air cleaners to prevent fuel evaporation. They actually shut the carburetors airtight when the engine isn't running. I also had Vern replace all the rubber hoses and lines in the cooling and fuel systems with aircraft-type steel lines. That was my contribution."

"It sounds like quite an involved operation!"

"Wait, it's not over yet! The halogen headlights have to be replaced by sealed-beam lights. There also has to be a seat-belt buzzer, and a buzzer that comes on when the door is open!"

"And a buzzer that comes on when you're going faster than fifty-five, right?"

"That'll probably come next!"

"Well, John, do you feel up to showing me how fast a Boxer can go? It should be safe out here in the middle of nowhere."

"Yes, probably. But I'll go slow."

He fires it up and takes it through the gears without straining it. We soon pass the 100-mph mark, still in fourth. I hardly feel the speed; the Boxer is as stable as a locomotive on its track. I enjoy the picture before my eyes; the all-tan, leather-covered interior, specially-upholstered for John, is a most pleasing place from which to watch the road and the grass as they rush toward me in out-of-focus streaks.

I become fascinated by the thought of the air that flows around the car, how it envelopes it and presses on it, and twirls and twists behind it. I imagine the air suddenly being split by the nose of the car, one stream flowing under it, and another, the stronger one, flowing up over the wide hood, pressing the car down, continuing across the windshield, over the roof, and then being split again, now by the aileron-spoiler mounted just behind the roof, allowing a small stream to escape down into the space behind the rear window, between the fins, to feed the hungry carburetors.

I feel the speed now! John is in fifth, still pressing on, still looking calm and collected, when he suddenly sees the only turning point within ten miles, the cross-road, come up only a few hundred yards away. He jumps on the brakes. The front sinks low, the rear lifts high, but the car stays steady on its track. We come to a stop, overshooting the cross-road by about fifty feet. Smoke bellows out from the wheel wells.

"The car has gone less than sixty miles, you know," said John. "It's only normal that the brakes smoke a little the first time you use them real hard!"

It takes my brain a moment to collect itself and formulate what I feel.

"One hundred and fifty-five miles per hour! You call that going slow?"

This view of the Boxer, top left, shows the dam below the grille and the vent in front of the rear wheel. Both were new elements that had been added to the 512 model. To the left, the luxurious cockpit, comfortable and surprisingly spacious. At the top of this page, John Dekker's Boxer is pictured while being towed to a waiting 747 at Rome airport for direct transportation to Los Angeles. Above, Dekker's car in the courtyard at the Factory. Notice how good the single color looks – a Dekker request. To the right, John Dekker during a tour of the Factory, captured beside a Boxer engine. (Photographs by Pininfarina, John Lamm and John Dekker, courtesy the Hilary Raab Collection and Road & Track.)

308 GTS

A Sculpture Of Speed

"It's the rake of the windshield," I told myself. "When the roof panel is removed, you can really see how much that windshield slopes," I mumbled as I bent down to examine the low silhouette of the car.

The white 308 Spyder reminded me of a sculpture on display. It looked like it had been placed there on the abandoned road by a committee of art lovers. The flowering desert west of Palm Springs, with its massive blue mountains and dramatic clouds, could not have been surpassed in beauty and grandeur by any exhibition complex in the world.

"It's the thin, pointed nose and the turned-up undercarriage," I continued, still talking to myself, still trying to pinpoint the reasons for the distinctive expression of speed in Pininfarina's Spyder design.

"It gives the car an appearance of lightness. Even when it stands still, it looks like it's flying. The speed theme is probably more pronounced in this than in any other design Pininfarina has done for Ferrari. The Boxer has it too, but in that design the element of power is the most prominent. With the Spyder, it's all speed," I reasoned to myself.

"It's the arrow-shape that does it, more than these individual isolated elements. That's what makes the Spyder look like it's always going full speed!" I concluded the discussion; but I immediately regretted having come to that conclusion. "That, and all the other things. They all work together!" I corrected myself, realizing that it was no easy task to decide what exactly makes a design work.

I stood up and walked over to the other side of the Spyder, where Chic Vandagriff and his son Cris were waiting. I had just taken the last shots of the car, and the sun was almost hidden behind the mountains to the west.

"Good-looking car!" Chic commented.

"It sure is!" I agreed. "The more you look, the better it gets. But what do you think — is it better-looking than, say, the Lusso?"

"It's too early to tell. The Lusso was very beautiful, but it belongs to a different era. It's always difficult to judge the classic qualities of a model while it's still in production. Nostalgia has a lot to do with the way we feel about a design, you know. One thing that I have always been impressed by, though — and I don't know how the Ferrari people do it — but they always manage to improve every new model, inside and out. The cars just get better and better!"

"Well, you should know!" I told him. "You've owned and driven all of them, haven't you?"

Chic Vandagriff, owner of Hollywood Sport Cars, and one of the first and most successful Ferrari dealers in the country, has deep roots in the world of automobiles. His grandfather was a riding mechanic for Barney Oldfield, and the feel for speed and excitement was transferred to Chic. He grew up in Burbank, a native Californian, and he spent the war years in high school. At the age of fifteen, after his father's untimely death, young Chic attempted to join the Navy. The age limit was seventeen, but he managed to get as far as the shipyard in San Diego before his actual age was discovered and he was sent home.

Without his father, the family had to manage on a limited income. But Chic wanted a car badly. He took to buying and selling horses, until he finally had enough money to get a 1931 Ford Model A Roadster. It didn't run, so Chic had to *make* it run! From then on his career was firmly connected with automobiles.

At the top left of the page, the flight-filled, uninterrupted profile of Pininfarina's 308 GTB, first seen at the Paris Salon in 1975. To the left, a bird's-eye comparison between the GTB and the GTS. The Spyder was introduced at the Frankfurt Show in 1977, and was received with much approval, immediately turning into a Ferrari best-seller. On this page, top, the European version of the four-seat 308 GT4, styled by Bertone and now replaced by the new Pininfarina-styled Mondial. Above and right, an interesting if not too successful attempt by Pininfarina to give the GTB a racing-machine look. This experiment was displayed at the 1977 Geneva Salon. (Photographs by Pininfarina, courtesy the Hilary Raab Collection and Ferrari S.p.A.)

"Yes, you're right! I've had just about all of the production cars," Chic said. "I liked them all, but I've always liked new cars. I traded for the new ones as soon as they came out. I guess that's natural when you're a dealer, but it also had to do with my background. I had my own clunker sales-lot when I was twenty-one, and I got plenty fed up with old beat-up cars!"

"It's quite a step from a used-car lot to a Ferrari dealership. How did it happen?" I asked.

"In the late fifties, when I worked as a salesman for a sports-car dealership in Burbank, I was able to buy an Austin-Healey 3000. I prepared it for racing and went to driver's school, then I drove it at Riverside and Willow Springs. At that time I got an offer to take over Hollywood Sport cars, and those responsibilities cut my racing career short. But I kept the Healey, hired a full-time racing mechanic, and got Ronnie Bucknum to drive it. We won thirty-five firsts and the Pacific Coast Cham-
(continued on overleaf)

S tyled in such a fashion as to reflect the looks of the 246 Dino as well as the Boxer, the 308 GT, powered by a vee-eight which was a further development of the original vee-six Dino engine, carries Ferrari's mid-engine concept into the eighties. The brand new Spyder pictured on these pages, chassis number 30101, was supplied by Hollywood Sport Cars of Hollywood, California. The early-evening sun filters through approaching clouds, casting soft shadows on Pininfarina's space-age sculpture – a striking contrast to the surrounding Palm Springs desert landscape.

pionship in 1962.

"It was during my years in racing that I first became involved with the early Ferrari enthusiasts on the West Coast — guys like Bill Doheny, John Edgar, Otto Zipper and others. At that time I also sold my first used Ferrari. I remember it well. It was a Boano. But it wasn't until 1964 that I began selling new Ferraris. That was the year of the Lusso. I drove one myself for a couple of years. Then, in 1965, I became the first of Bill Harrah's dealers when he took over the Ferrari distributorship for the West Coast. I got myself a GTS at that time."

"I've heard that you have a very good relationship with the Factory, and that you even took classes in Italian to be able to communicate better with them," I said. "When did you first go there for a visit?"

"I went there for the first time in 1968. I met Amerigo Manicardi then, Ferrari's commercial director in charge of sales and marketing. I count him as one of my best friends. I also met Ferrari himself at that time. I might tell you something of interest that happened on one of my trips to the Factory. I know Ferrari claims not to speak or understand English, but I think he does! How else can you explain this?

"We were sitting around a table in the restaurant across the street from the Factory, having lunch. Ferrari, Manicardi, Gozzi, and many others were there, among them the organizers from Le Mans. Ferrari kept up an involved discussion with them in French. Everybody talked to each other about something. I talked to Gozzi in English. I told him about a new race car that Jerry Titus and I were developing that had no suspension. When I said that, Ferrari, without interrupting the conversation with the Le Mans people, leaned across to Gozzi and asked him in Italian to please take notes, because he wanted to know all about this race car that didn't have any suspension. I was impressed. Not only was he able to keep up a detailed discussion in French, but he was also aware of everything else that was being said around the table. I got the impression that it didn't matter whether it was said in English, Italian or French — he heard and understood it all!"

"Have you seen him lately?" I asked.

"I last saw him in 1978, in his office at the test track by the Factory. He's getting older, like everyone else, but he's as vigorous and sharp as ever. Still going strong!"

"During your visits to Italy, did you drive Ferraris, or did you drive Fiats, like Mister Ferrari does?"

"Sometimes I drove Ferraris. I remember one time especially well; it was during my first visit in 1968. I drove a 275 GTB/4 that time. I remember taking it on a trip to Naples. On the way back to Modena, I drove the Auto-

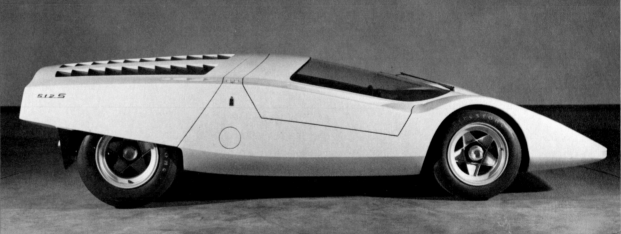

Pininfarina has, over the past three decades, held a virtual monopoly on formulating the Ferrari look. Featured on these pages are styling exercises that show what could have become — and what will become? At the top of this page, the engine-less P6, displayed in 1968 at the Turin Show. The Boxer and the 308 GTB lines can already be detected. Above, the most exciting of them all, the 512 S, featured at the Turin Show in 1969. To the right, top, the Modulo, unveiled at the Geneva Salon in 1970. Right, the 1974 Cr 25, photographed in Pininfarina's wind tunnel. To the left, its extremely well-designed interior. (Photographs by Pininfarina, courtesy the Hilary Raab Collection.)

strada. I made it in less than five hours, which works out to an average of about 165 mph. When I told Manicardi about it, he just looked at me with a stone face and asked what had caused the delay. It's true, by the way; Ferrari does drive a Fiat. Well, nowadays he's chauffeured — in a Fiat!"

"You've been a Ferrari dealer for fifteen years now. Has the excitement worn off?" I asked.

"The best way to answer that question, I guess, is to tell you of an experience I had at the Factory, also in 1968. One of the first Daytonas off the production line was sitting there ready for preferred delivery. It had Chinetti's name written in big letters on the windshield. I asked what I had to do to get that kind of treatment. The answer was, 'You have to be our man for twenty years, like Chinetti!' I still remember those words.

"Yes, I've been at it for fifteen years. But I still have the ambition to improve. I'm talking about areas like customer relations, sales volume, Factory relations, service and so on. My contacts with the Factory are already excellent; for instance, I'm one of the first to see the new models, and I often have the opportunity to influence things in a small way. Another step I've taken recently is to put Cris in charge of the Service Department. To say it all in one sentence: my goal is to become better and better — just like the Ferraris!"

He opened the door and sat down in the open cockpit. I knew he had a dealers' meeting to attend in Palm Springs that night. The shooting had taken longer than expected, and I could see he was anxious to leave. I just wanted to get in one last question.

"With all the Ferraris that have passed through your hands, have you kept any of them?"

"Yes, I still have a 365 GTC/4. I really liked that car. Cris is almost done with the restoration. Well, I guess I have to be on my way now. You'll go back to Hollywood with Cris, right? See you!"

The vee-eight came to life with a well-muffled but unquestionably exotic sound. The racing heritage could not be hidden behind a set of mufflers. He drove off, taking it easy at first, then sped up, turning east toward Palm Springs. The car soon disappeared beyond the fields of yellow desert flowers, but its sound hung in the air awhile longer.

"It's really funny," Cris said with a smile. "That GTC is mine. He gave it to me a couple of years ago; he said I could have it if I restored it. Now, when it's almost finished, he gets excited and thinks it's his. I'll have to remind him!"

"I didn't think he liked old cars."

"He does — when they're like new!"

"Ferraris For the Road," fifth in the Survivors Series, was photographed, written and designed by Henry Rasmussen. The Model Resumés in the content section, as well as the Chronology of Production, were written by Larry Crane. Assistant designer was Walt Woesner. Copy editors were Barbara Harold and Kathy O'Brien. Typesetting was supplied by Tintype of San Luis Obispo. The color separations were produced by Graphic Arts Systems of Burbank. Zellerbach Paper Company supplied the 100-pound Flokote stock, manufactured by S.D. Warren. The special inks were formulated by Spectrum Ink Company, Los Angeles. LithoCraft of Anaheim printed the book, under the supervision of Brad Thurman. The binding was provided by National Bindery of Pomona. In addition to the skilled craftsmen associated with these firms, the author wishes to thank the owners for their time and enthusiasm.

Special acknowledgements go to Larry Crane of Santa Barbara, for his excellent writing and invaluable help with technical information; to Hilary Raab of Chicago, for supplying the majority of the black and white photos from his extensive collection in such an unselfish manner; to Cris Vandagriff of Hollywood Sport Cars, for his inspiring support and inventiveness in locating cars; to Tom Warth of Motorbooks International, without whose actions of confidence this book would not have been done.

The author also wishes to thank Tony Anthony, Dean Batchelor, Steve Earle, John Gaughan, John Hajduk, Vern Lindholm of Ferrari Compliance in Santa Ana, Mike Lynch, Tom Martindale, Larry Menser, Ed Niles, Giancarlo Perini, Chuck Queener, Robert Resler of Rapid Color in Glendale, Dyke Ridgley, Chuck Smith of Road & Track, Henry Smith, and Henry Wolf.